Stanford Achievement Test

A Test Prep Program

Book 1

Columbus, OH

The McGraw-Hill Companies

www.sra4kids.com

SRA

Printed in the United States of America.

Send all inquiries to:
SRA/McGraw-Hill
4400 Easton Commons
Columbus, OH 43219

ISBN 0-07-584094-4

12 13 14 RMN 12 11 10

Book 1 On Your Way to

Scoring High Stanford Achievement Test

Name ______________________________

Unit 1

Word Study Skills

Lesson 1a Word Study Skills

SAMPLE A

- ◯ window
- ◯ sidewalk
- ◯ cleaning

SAMPLE B

- ◯ closest
- ◯ closed
- ◯ closer

If you are not sure which answer choice is correct, take your best guess.

1
- ◯ feather
- ◯ notebook
- ◯ purple

2
- ◯ horseshoe
- ◯ ringing
- ◯ kitchen

3
- ◯ letter
- ◯ warning
- ◯ armchair

STOP 

4
- ◯ lands
- ◯ landing
- ◯ landed

5
- ◯ nicely
- ◯ nicest
- ◯ nicer

6
- ◯ even
- ◯ ever
- ◯ evening

STOP 

SAMPLE C
she'll
she's
she'd

7
doesn't
didn't
don't

8
weren't
wasn't
won't

9
we'll
we've
we're

SAMPLE D
both
hop
rope
for

10
trip
thick
train
smart

11
flew
were
weed
shoe

12
bird
order
drink
dark

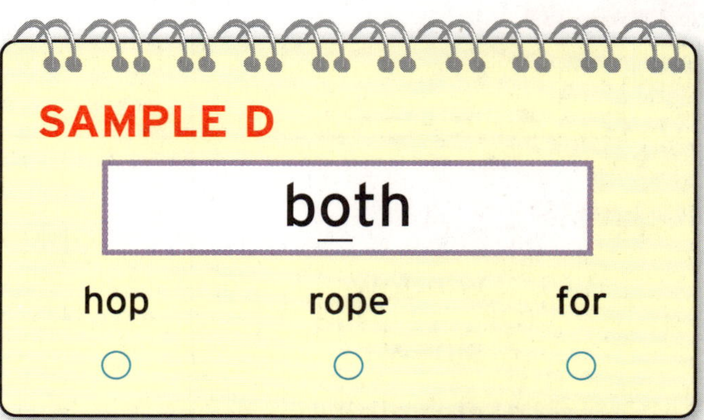

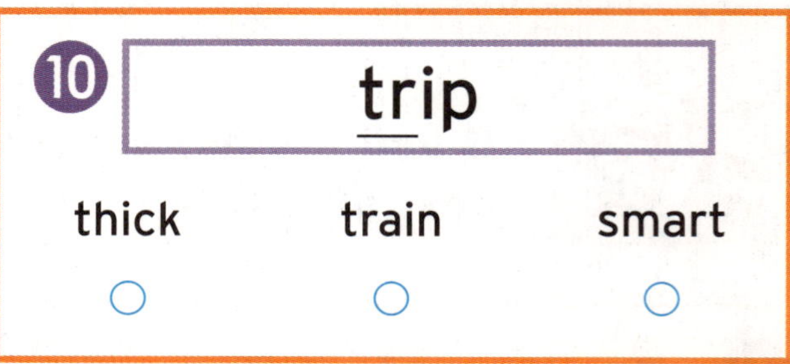

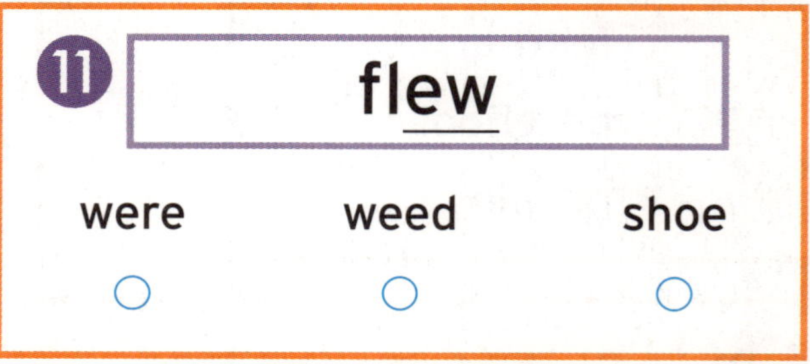

STOP

GO

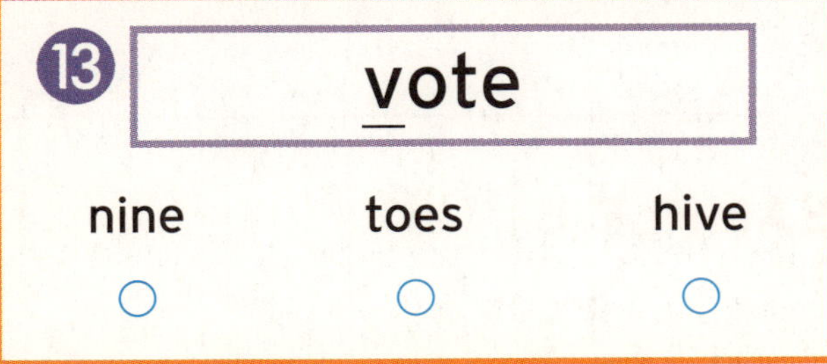

13 **vote**

nine ○ toes ○ hive ○

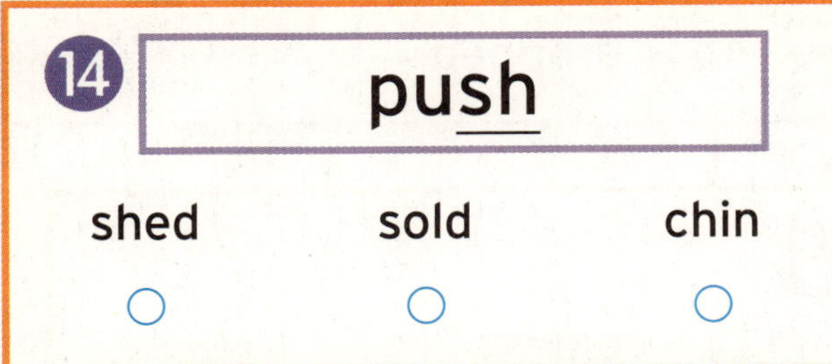

14 **push**

shed ○ sold ○ chin ○

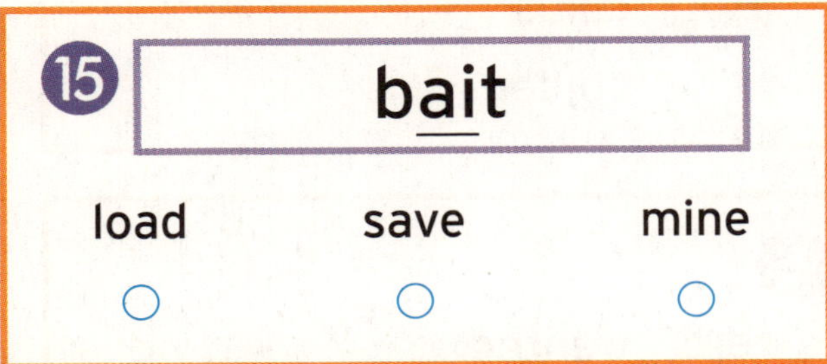

15 **bait**

load ○ save ○ mine ○

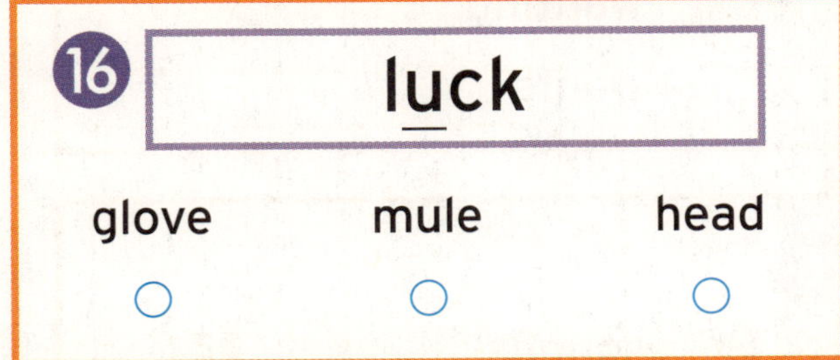

16 **luck**

glove ○ mule ○ head ○

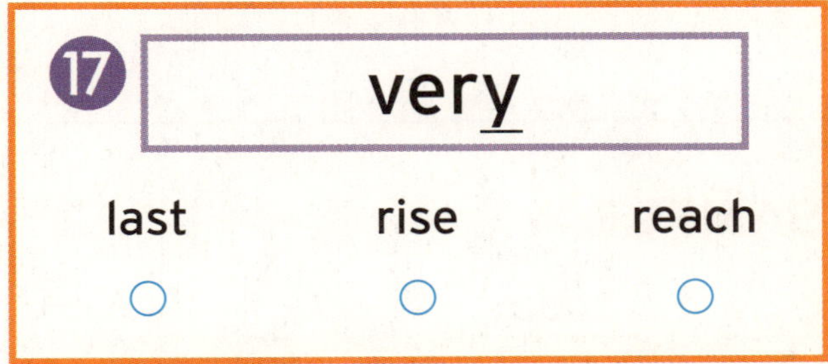

17 **very**

last ○ rise ○ reach ○

18 **torn**

bird ○ hunt ○ fort ○

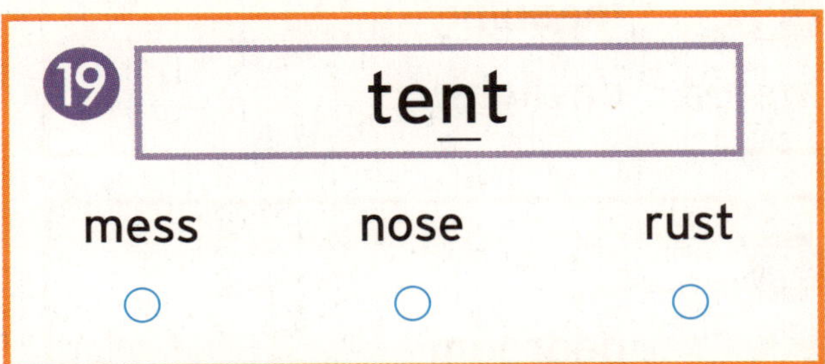

19 **tent**

mess ○ nose ○ rust ○

20 **foot**

hope ○ roar ○ stood ○

STOP

Word Study Skills

Lesson 1b Word Study Skills

SAMPLE A

- ○ today
- ○ somewhere
- ○ almost

SAMPLE B

- ○ drops
- ○ dropping
- ○ dropped

1

- ○ weather
- ○ meaning
- ○ daylight

2

- ○ bedroom
- ○ looking
- ○ highest

3

- ○ supper
- ○ playground
- ○ repeat

4

- ○ coldest
- ○ colds
- ○ colder

5

- ○ wanted
- ○ wanting
- ○ wants

6

- ○ sounds
- ○ sounded
- ○ sounding

STOP

STOP

SAMPLE C
you've
you're
you'll

7
shouldn't
couldn't
wouldn't

8
they've
they're
they'll

9
we'll
we've
we're

STOP

SAMPLE D
much
reach
with
bank

10
close
open
cloud
stop

11
best
hear
chew
men

12
frost
afraid
raft
force

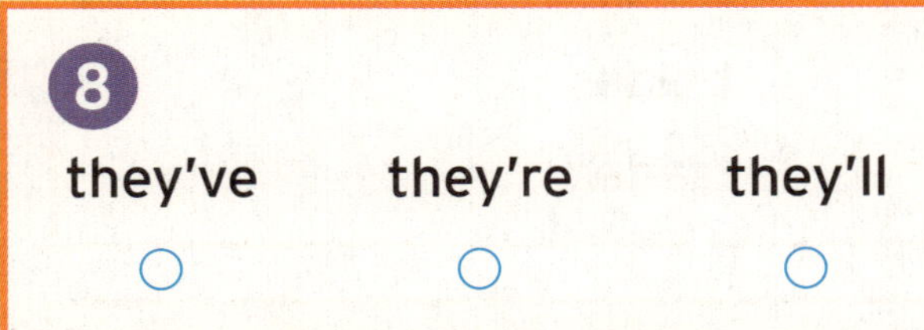

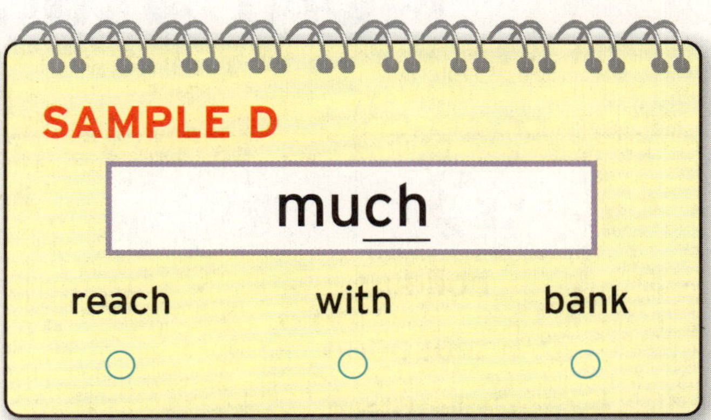

STOP

Unit 1

Test Yourself: Word Study Skills

SAMPLE A

- ○ holiday
- ○ teaspoon
- ○ trouble

SAMPLE B

- ○ smiling
- ○ smiles
- ○ smiled

1

- ○ eleven
- ○ problem
- ○ firewood

2

- ○ raincoat
- ○ weather
- ○ distant

3

- ○ shinier
- ○ everything
- ○ thirsty

STOP

4

- ○ trading
- ○ trades
- ○ traded

5

- ○ careless
- ○ carefully
- ○ careful

6

- ○ drawing
- ○ draws
- ○ drawn

STOP

Unit
1

SAMPLE C
I'm
I'll
I've

7
she'd
she'll
she's

8
we'll
we've
we'd

9
you'd
you've
you're

SAMPLE D
just
lunch
sure
hour

10
game
judge
leg
stop

11
share
park
load
pair

12
cloth
thank
lost
closet

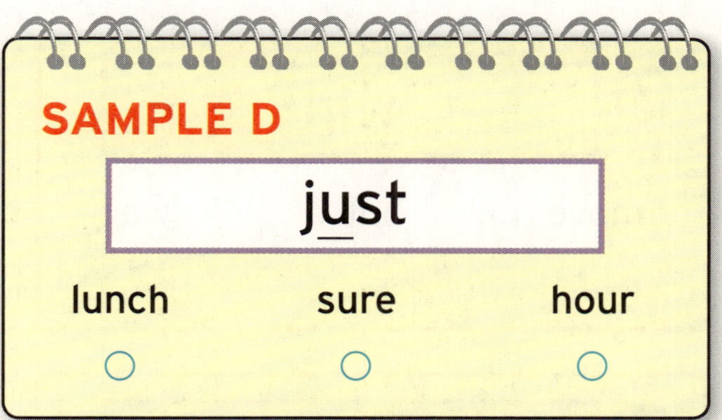

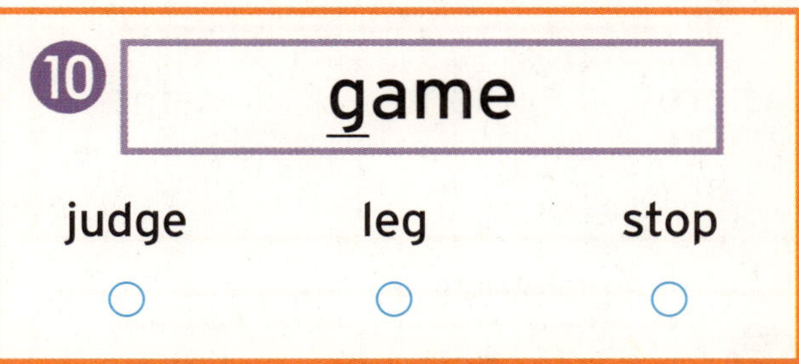

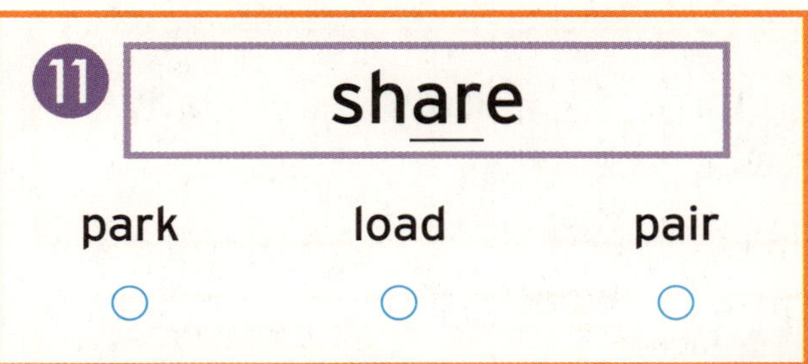

STOP

GO

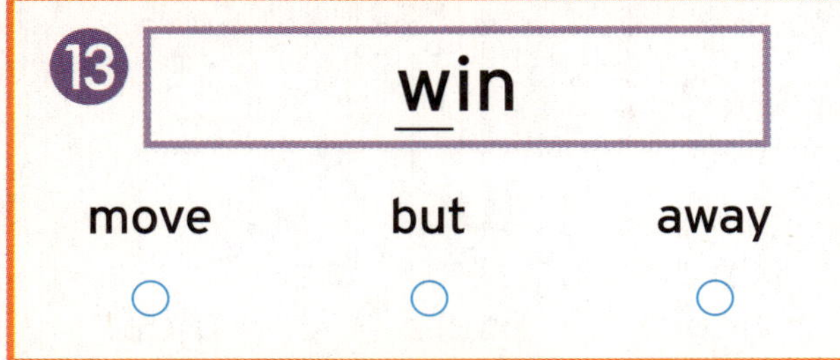

13 **win**

move ○ but ○ away ○

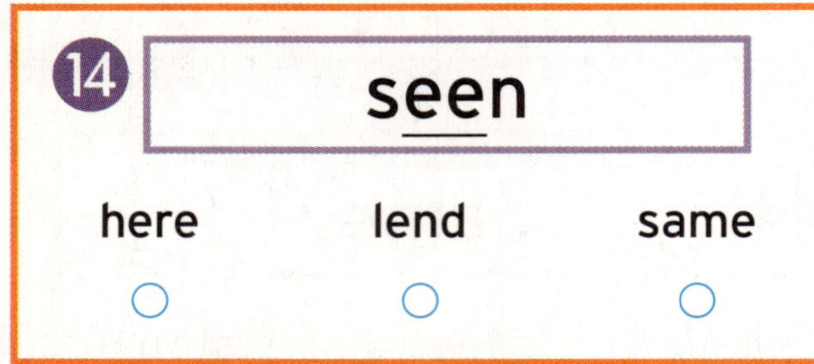

14 **seen**

here ○ lend ○ same ○

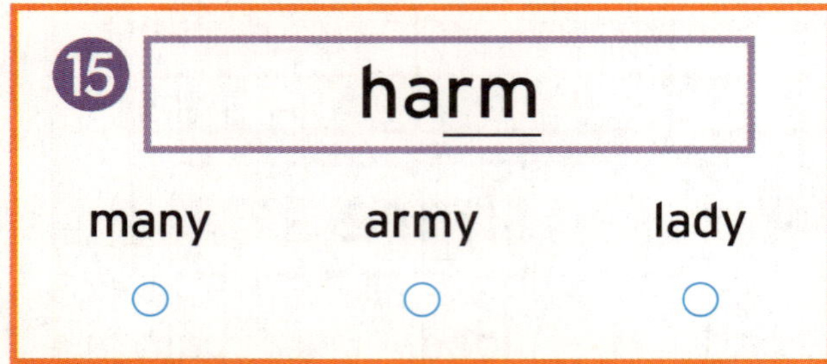

15 **harm**

many ○ army ○ lady ○

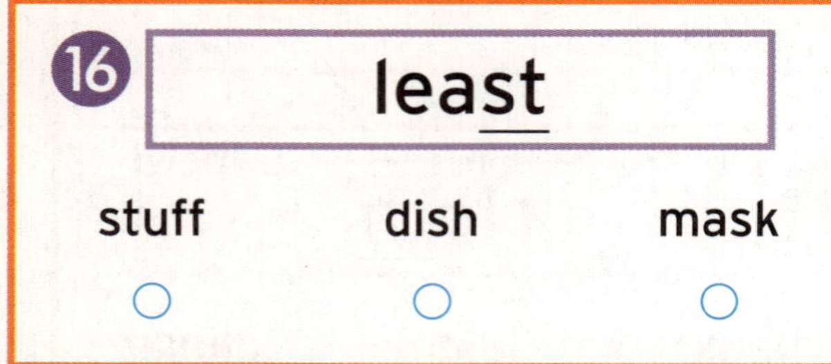

16 **least**

stuff ○ dish ○ mask ○

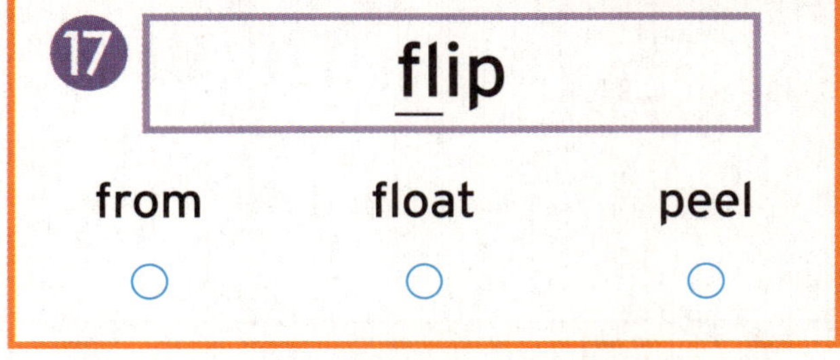

17 **flip**

from ○ float ○ peel ○

18 **rub**

snow ○ clap ○ iron ○

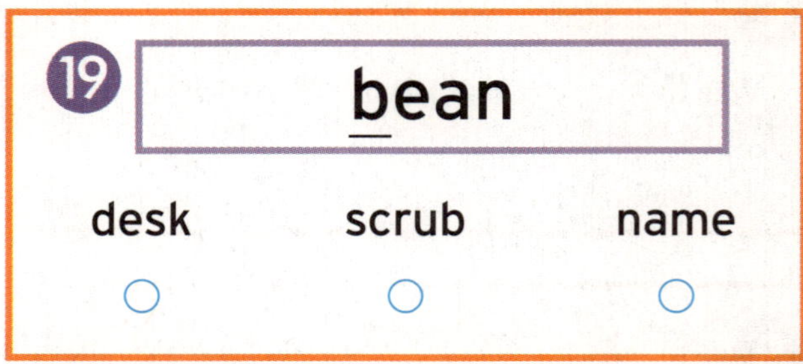

19 **bean**

desk ○ scrub ○ name ○

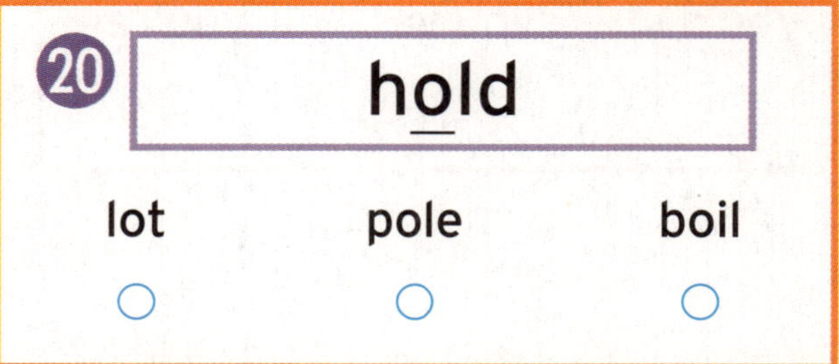

20 **hold**

lot ○ pole ○ boil ○

STOP

Unit 2

Word Reading

Lesson 2a Word Reading

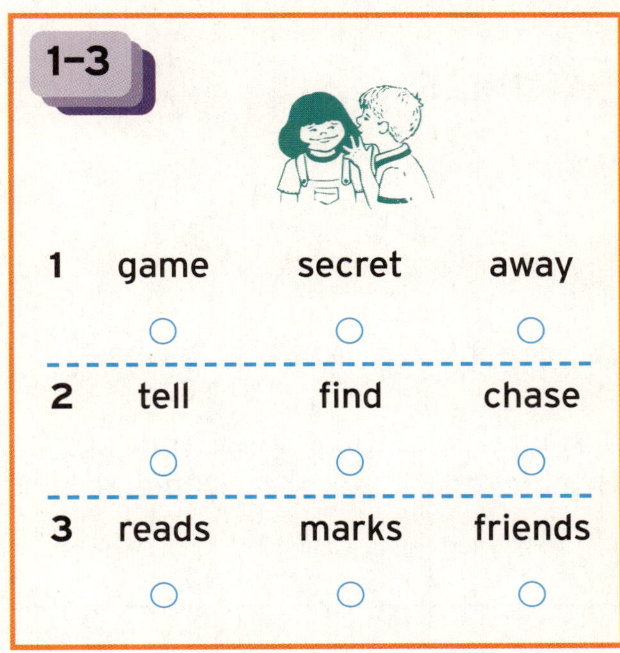

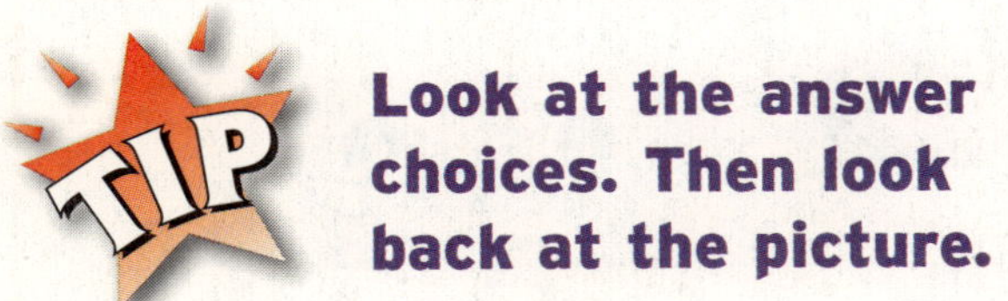

Look at the answer choices. Then look back at the picture.

STOP

Word Reading

Lesson 2b **Word Reading**

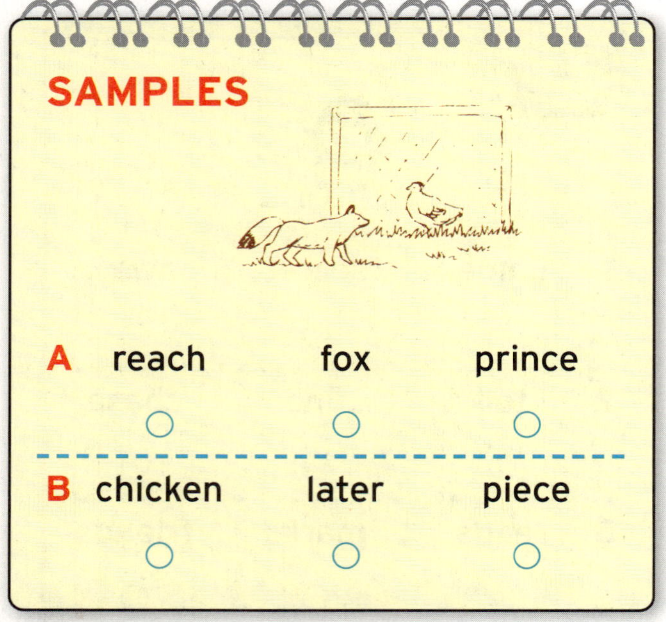

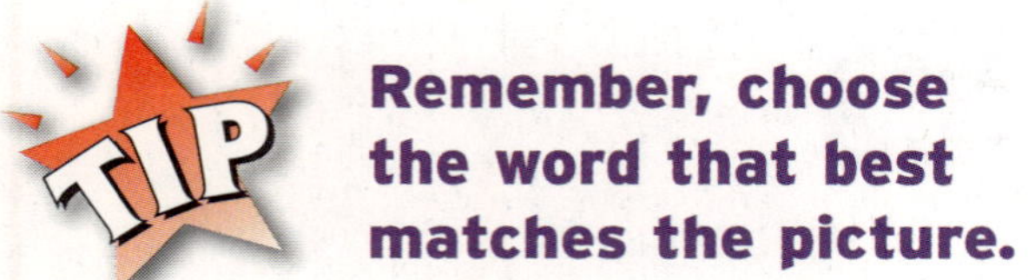

Remember, choose the word that best matches the picture.

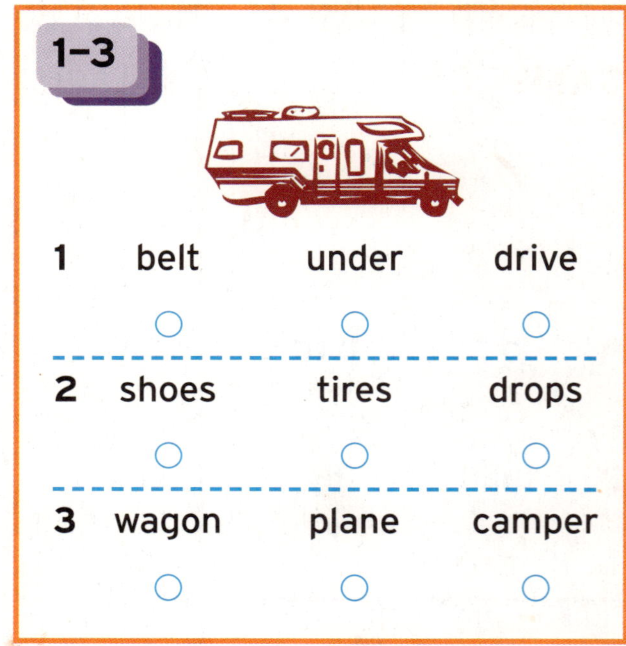

4-6

4	night	family	main
5	band	pen	meal
6	eat	rush	horse

Unit 2

Test Yourself: Word Reading

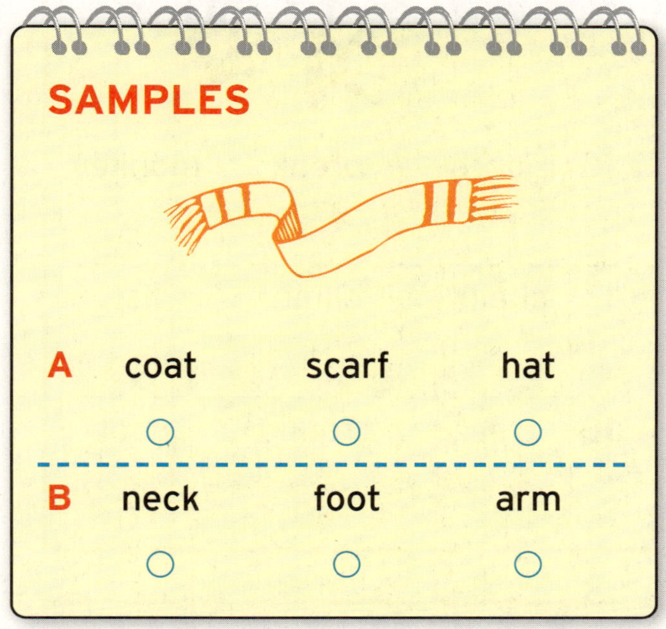

SAMPLES

A	coat ○	scarf ○	hat ○
B	neck ○	foot ○	arm ○

1–3

1	tools ○	toys ○	books ○
2	run ○	fly ○	dig ○
3	floor ○	kitchen ○	yard ○

4–6

4	write ○	paint ○	read ○
5	brush ○	spoon ○	comb ○
6	sky ○	dirt ○	color ○

7–9

7	drop ○	carry ○	write ○
8	shoes ○	letter ○	shoe ○
9	pen ○	car ○	bus ○

GO →

10–12

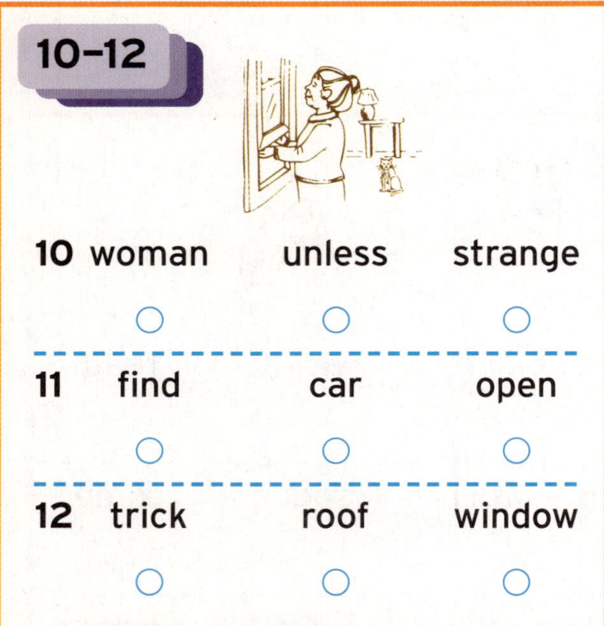

10	woman ○	unless ○	strange ○
11	find ○	car ○	open ○
12	trick ○	roof ○	window ○

16–18

16	month ○	break ○	monkey ○
17	chain ○	climb ○	list ○
18	tree ○	ground ○	pool ○

13–15

13	field ○	pond ○	forest ○
14	frog ○	reason ○	frost ○
15	watch ○	them ○	swim ○

19–21

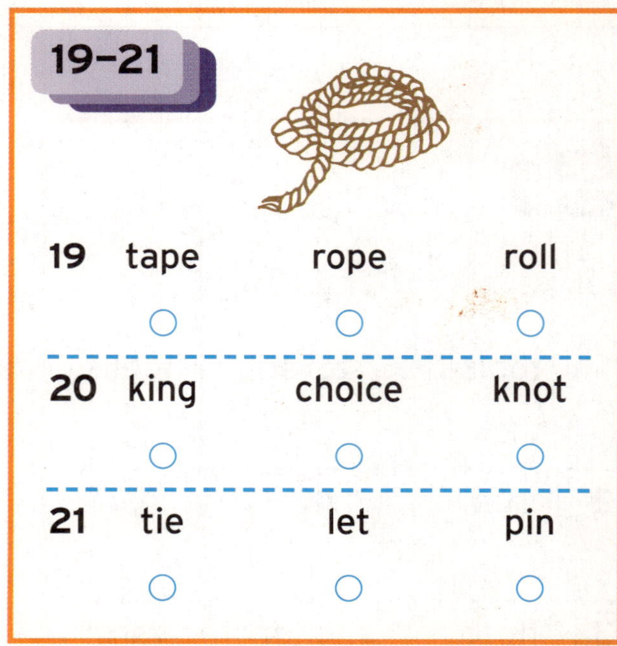

19	tape ○	rope ○	roll ○
20	king ○	choice ○	knot ○
21	tie ○	let ○	pin ○

STOP

Reading Comprehension

Lesson 3a Sentence Comprehension

SAMPLE A

Then she went home.

Listen carefully to the sentences you hear or read. Think about what they mean before you pick your answer.

1 His fur is nice and soft.

STOP

SAMPLE B

Let's go sit under the tree.

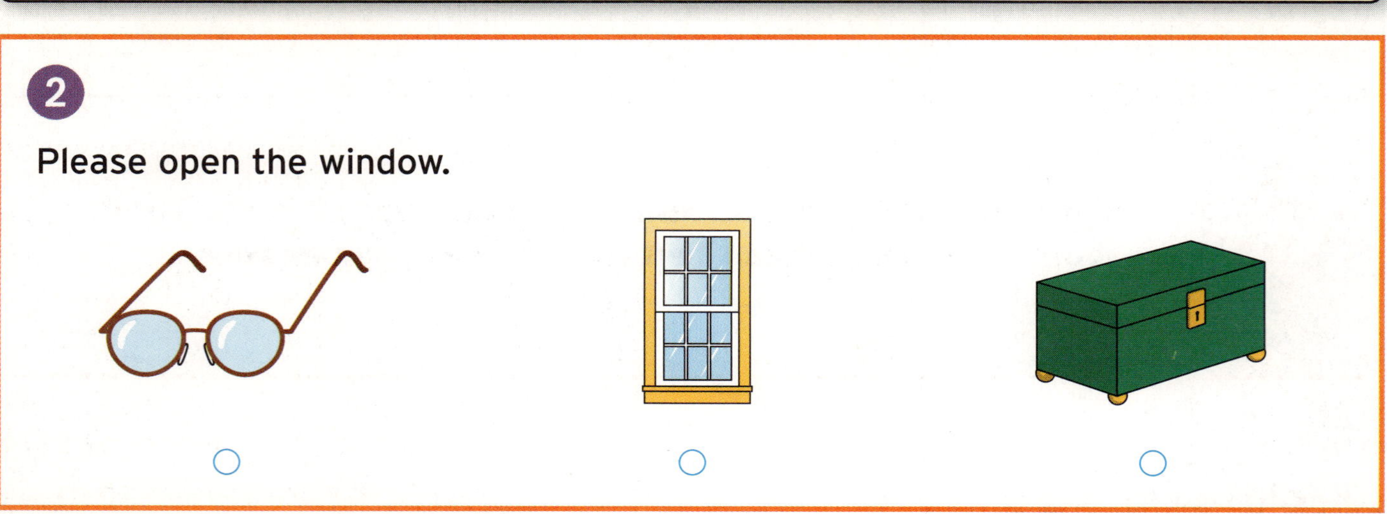

2

Please open the window.

3

It's hot. I need something to drink.

STOP 

Reading Comprehension

Lesson 3b Sentence Comprehension

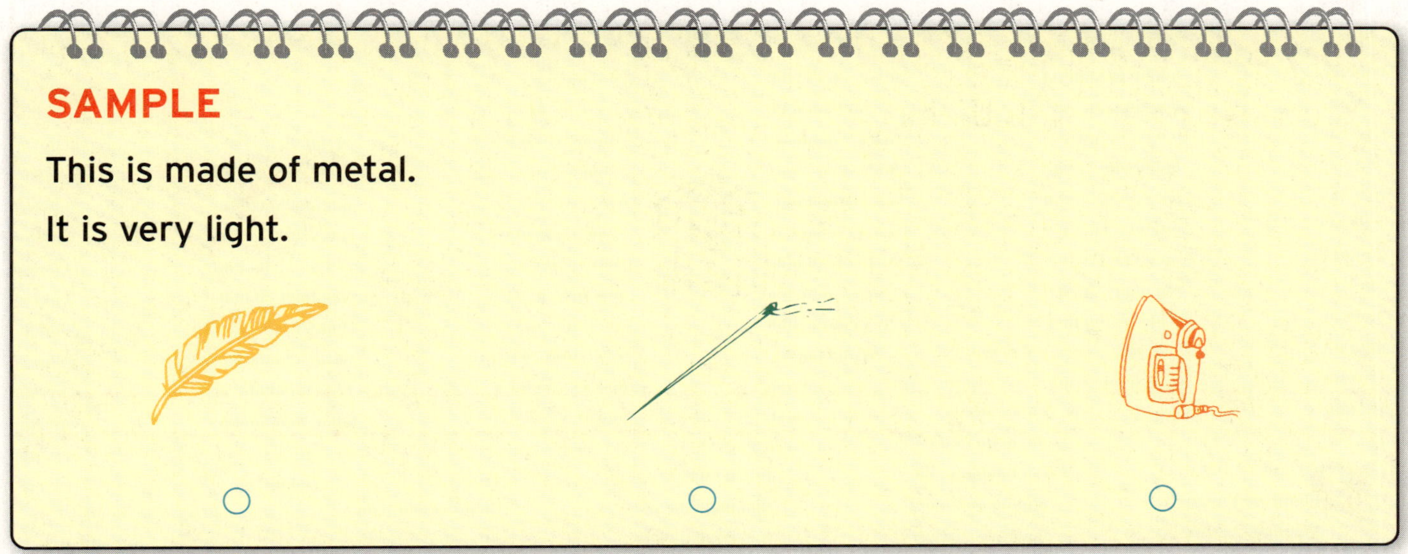

SAMPLE

This is made of metal.

It is very light.

Look back at the picture to find the answer.

1

You can blow it.

It makes noise.

GO

They come in a box.

You make colors with them.

It is in the ocean.

It looks like a star.

It has a long handle.

You use it for leaves.

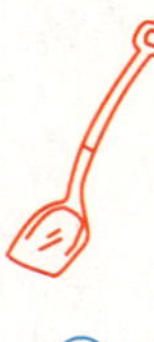  

STOP

Unit 3

Reading Comprehension

Lesson 4a Story Comprehension

SAMPLES

Nature Walks

Bill and his brother like to walk in the woods. They look at the leaves on the trees. Sometimes they pick up pinecones. They often see birds flying around. Small animals run away when the boys come close.

SAMPLE A

When they walk in the woods, the boys are

- ○ angry
- ○ happy
- ○ scared

SAMPLE B

The boys seem to like

- ○ nature
- ○ cars
- ○ sports

Look back at the story to find the right answer.

GO

Tugboats

A tugboat is small, but it does an important job. It helps big ships unload. Big ships carry things across the oceans. They have to go into harbors on the shore to unload. The big ships must sail into small places that they do not know well. They could run into something. The tugboat can push or pull the big ship safely into harbor. Tugs are strong and work very hard. A small tugboat can make sure a large ship gets into the harbor safely.

1. A tugboat is like a
   - ○ helper
   - ○ harbor
   - ○ truck

2. Tugboats make sure that ships are
   - ○ fast
   - ○ big
   - ○ safe

3. A tugboat's job is
   - ○ silly
   - ○ important
   - ○ easy

GO

Animals

Animals can live in very cold places. They have different ways of staying warm. Feathers keep birds warm. Thick fur covers some animals, like bears. A layer of fat also helps bears and other animals stay warm. In cold places, all the animals find a way to keep themselves warm.

4. This story tells some ways that animals

○ catch food
○ stay warm
○ find homes

5. Bears keep warm with

○ only fur
○ only fat
○ fur and fat

Tim and Dusty

Sometimes my dog, Dusty, and I go to my uncle's farm. We play chase in the big green fields. When I am tired, we go to the corral to help feed the horses. Then we chase each other again.

6. Tim likes to visit the farm so he can

○ swim
○ run
○ climb

7. The corral must be where the horses

○ live
○ eat
○ sleep

STOP 

Reading Comprehension

Lesson 4b Story Comprehension

SAMPLES

Annie and the Circus

Annie's friend invited her to go to the circus. It was in a big tent. The tent was full of people. There was music playing. Three large rings were in the middle of the tent. Different acts were in each ring. Annie did not know where to look first. She loved the animals. Her friend liked the clowns best. Later the girls played circus. They made-believe they were part of the acts.

SAMPLE A

Annie thought the best part was the

- ○ clowns
- ○ music
- ○ animals

SAMPLE B

Where was the circus?

- ○ In a mall
- ○ In a tent
- ○ In a school

If a question seems hard, skip it and come back to it later.

GO

Elephants

Elephants can talk to each other. They do not use words like we do. They move their big floppy ears. They raise their long trunks in the air and wave them about. Elephants talk by moving their bodies. They can also make noises. One loud sound is called trumpeting. Elephants lift their trunks in the air when they make this sound. They sometimes make grunting sounds. Mothers seem to talk to their children with these noises. We do not understand what the elephants are saying. Scientists are trying to learn what elephants are saying.

1. How do elephants talk?
   - ○ With words
   - ○ With noises and grunts
   - ○ By running and jumping

2. When elephants trumpet, they
   - ○ lift their trunks in the air
   - ○ stomp their feet on the ground
   - ○ move from side to side

3. Elephants do not
   - ○ lift their trunks
   - ○ move their ears
   - ○ use words

GO 

Games at the Park

Jenny picked up her new bat and walked to the park. Her friends, Sarah and Henry, were waiting for her.

"Hello," said Jenny. "Are you ready to play baseball?"

"We thought we were going to play soccer today, Jenny," answered Sarah.

"That's right," said Henry. "Soccer is fun."

"Let's play baseball today," said Jenny "I want to use my new bat. Then we can play soccer tomorrow."

Together, the three friends played baseball all afternoon.

4 What game did Jenny want to play?

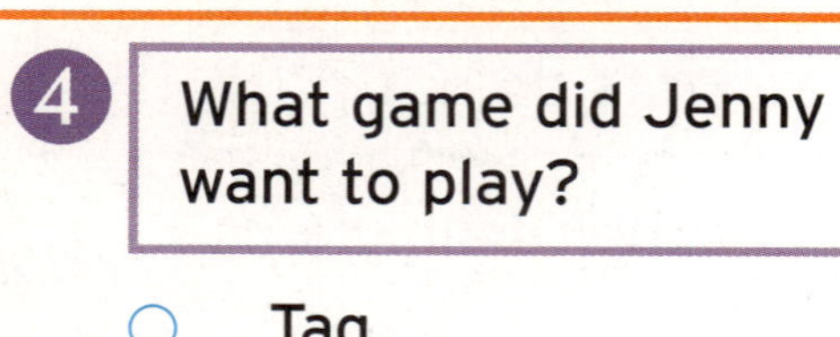

- ○ Tag
- ○ Baseball
- ○ Hide-and-seek

5 Jenny has a new

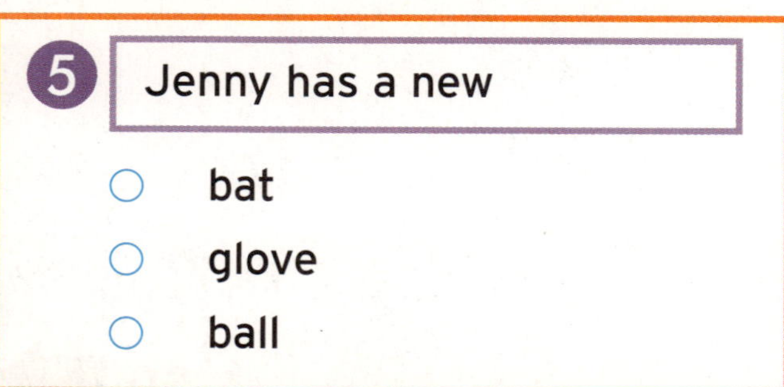

- ○ bat
- ○ glove
- ○ ball

6 Tomorrow, Jenny and her friends will

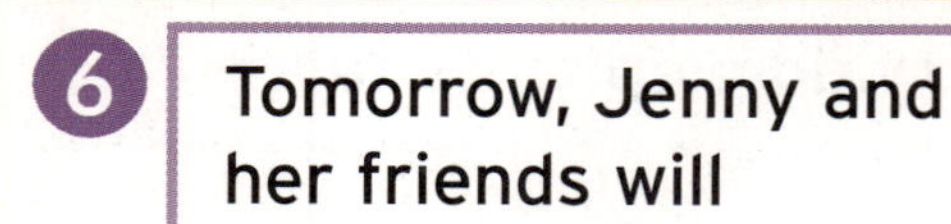

- ○ play soccer
- ○ go swimming
- ○ read books

STOP

Unit 3

Test Yourself: Reading Comprehension

STOP

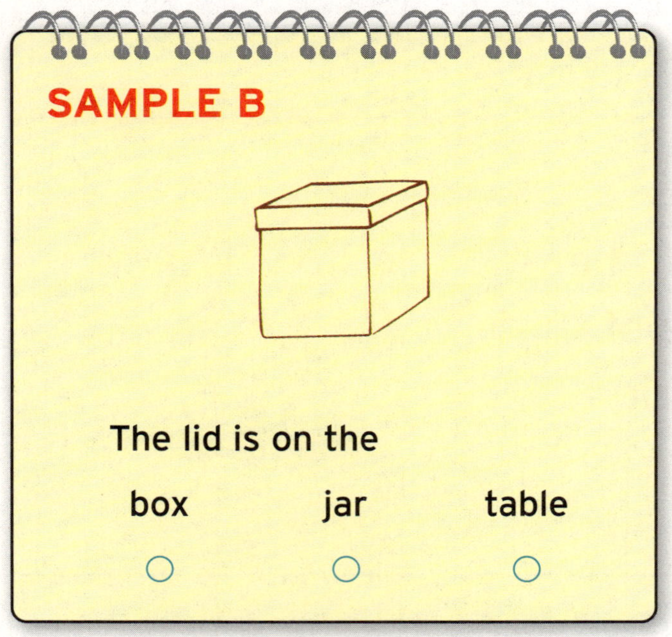

SAMPLE B

The lid is on the

box	jar	table
○	○	○

2–4

2 The girl is

walking	standing	sitting
○	○	○

3 She is

mixing	baking	carrying
○	○	○

4 something in a

pot	bowl	dish
○	○	○

STOP

Tom's New Home

"You have too many cats, Amy," her mother said. "You must find new homes for some of them." Amy was sad, but she knew her mother was right.

One day, Amy's aunt came to visit. "I will take a cat home with me," she said. "I would like to have a cat."

Amy caught Tom, her newest cat, and put him in a box. Amy put the box in the car. Then Aunt Patricia drove Tom to her home. Tom had a new home. Aunt Patricia had a new friend.

SAMPLE C

Tom was a

- ○ dog
- ○ bird
- ○ cat

SAMPLE D

Amy did not want to

- ○ keep all her cats
- ○ give her cats away
- ○ visit with Aunt Patricia

GO

Friends

Bear is a big, white dog. Leo is a small, gray cat. They are best friends. They live at the same house. Some people think cats and dogs do not get along together. These two animals like each other very much. They even eat out of the same dish at the same time.

Some people think they cannot get along with other people who are different. If people spent some time together, they might get to know each other better. If they knew each other better, they might become friends. Wouldn't it be nice if people could be friends the way Bear and Leo are friends?

5 This story tells about

- ○ people who are friends
- ○ taking care of pets
- ○ animals who are friends

6 The small gray cat is named

- ○ Leo
- ○ Bear
- ○ Friend

7 The first step in becoming friends is

- ○ eating together
- ○ spending time together
- ○ having dog and cat pets

Raising Money

Terry went to a fair at the park. The people in Terry's town wanted to help pay for a new swimming pool. There were rides and games. A band played music.

Terry read the menu at the food stand. He wanted something to eat.

MENU

Sandwiches 50¢

Juice 25¢

Milk 25¢

Fruit 25¢

Cookies 25¢

8 Which item on the food menu cost the most?

- ○ Milk
- ○ Fruit
- ○ Sandwiches

9 The fair was held to raise money to build a

- ○ swimming pool
- ○ park
- ○ public library

GO

Juan's Room

Juan had a nice room all to himself. He had toys, books, and a place to hang his clothes. Juan's mother wanted him to keep the room clean. Juan did not like to pick up his things.

One day, Juan started to get dressed. There were no clean clothes to wear to school that day. "What did I ask you to do with your dirty clothes, Juan?" asked his mother. "Did you pick them up? I have some clothes for you to wear today. Next time there may not be any."

Juan remembered how it felt when he had no clean clothes. He picked up his clothes. He also picked up his other things.

10 Juan was surprised when he

- ○ had no clothes for school
- ○ couldn't find his games
- ○ picked up his clothes

11 What lesson did Juan learn?

- ○ To pick up his clothes and things
- ○ To let his mother pick up his things
- ○ To wash his own clothes

GO

Lemonade

Eliza and her little brother, Dan, like to make lemonade. Eliza cuts the lemons in half. She and Dan squeeze the lemons until their hands are tired. Then Eliza pours the lemon juice into a big pitcher, picks out the seeds, then adds water. Dan adds sugar with a measuring cup, while Eliza stirs the juice. Finally, Eliza puts in some ice cubes to make the lemonade cold. Then they drink big glasses of fresh lemonade.

12 The first step is to

- ○ add sugar
- ○ pour the juice
- ○ cut the lemons

13 Eliza and Dan's hands get tired from

- ○ squeezing lemons
- ○ stirring juice
- ○ picking out seeds

14 A measuring cup is used for the

- ○ sugar
- ○ juice
- ○ ice cubes

STOP

Unit 4

Mathematics Problem Solving

Lesson 5a Problem Solving

SAMPLE

41	51	31	4110	1041
	○	●	○	○

Listen carefully for important words. Look at the problem while you listen.

1

$7 + \square = 7$

1	7	0	14
○	○	●	○

2

254	425	542	105
●	○	○	○

3

○

○

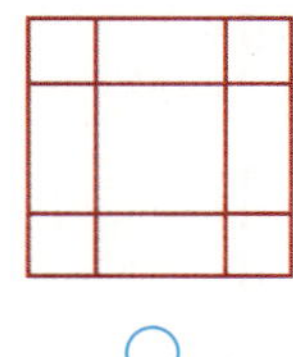

○

●

GO

IN GOD WE TRUST
LIBERTY
LIBERTY
IN GOD WE TRUST
LIBERTY
IN GOD WE TRUST

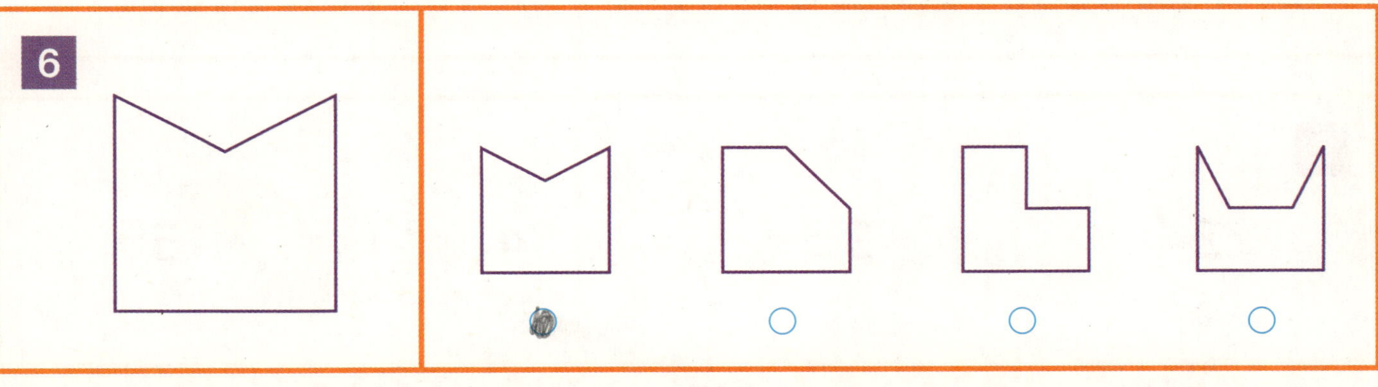

GO

PETS

Grade 1					
Grade 2					
Grade 3					
Grade 4					
Grade 5					

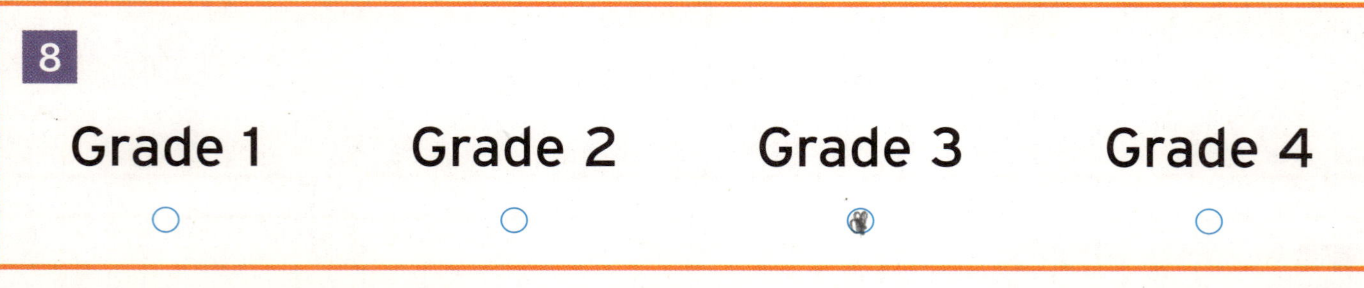

GO

11

JUNE

S	M	T	W	T	F	S
	1	2	3	4	5	6
7	8	9	10	11	12	13
14	15	16	17	18	19	20
21	22	23	24	25	26	27
28	29	30				

June 2 ○ June 9 ○ June 15 ○ June 16 ○

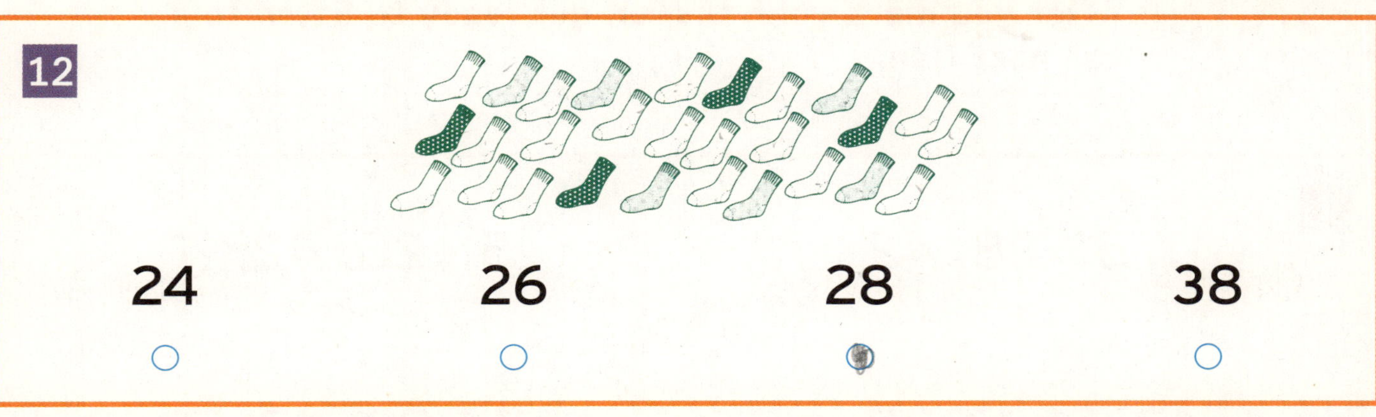

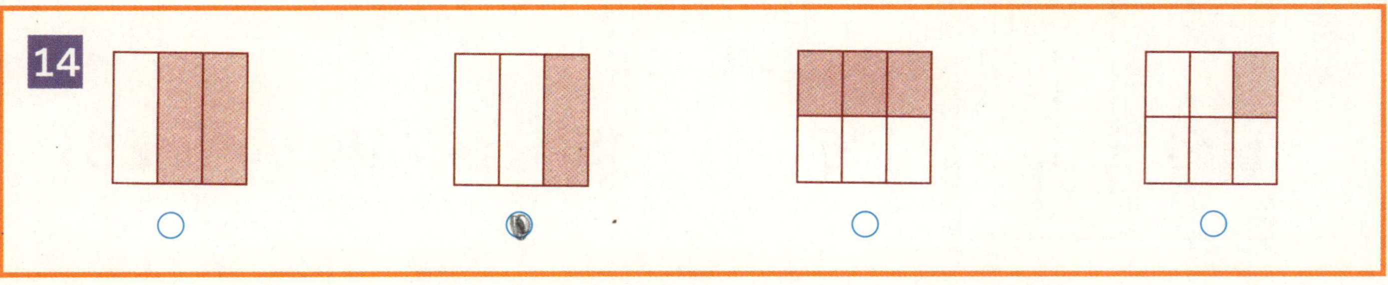

STOP

Mathematics Problem Solving

Lesson 5b Problem Solving

SAMPLE

760 ○ 706 ○ 76 ○ 67 ○

After you mark your answer, get ready to listen to the next item.

1

17, 51, 28, 42 ○

51, 28, 42, 17 ○

42, 51, 17, 28 ○

17, 28, 42, 51 ○

2

FARM ANIMALS

10 ○ 15 ○ 18 ○ 28 ○

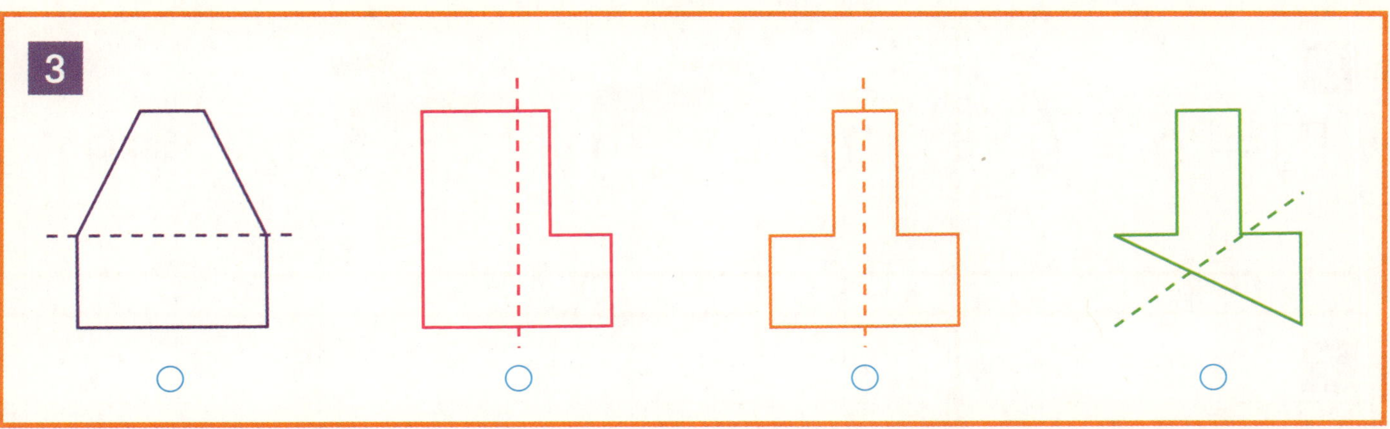

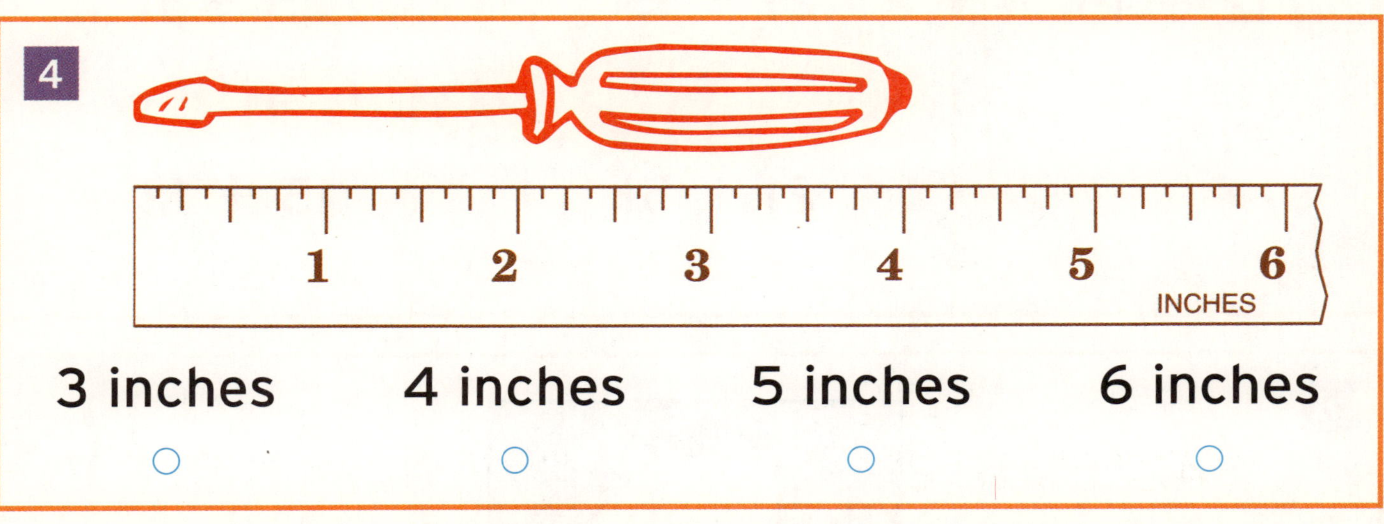

GO

6

$\square + 9 = 9$

0	1	9	99
○	○	○	○

7

$12 + 15$

$21 + 15$ ○	$25 + 11$ ○
$21 + 51$ ○	$15 + 12$ ○

8

○

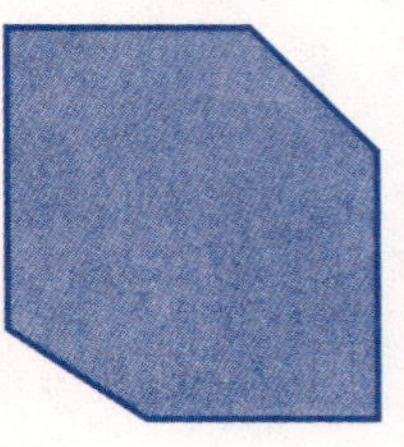
○

○

○

GO

9

pounds ○ gallons ○ cups ○ miles ○

10

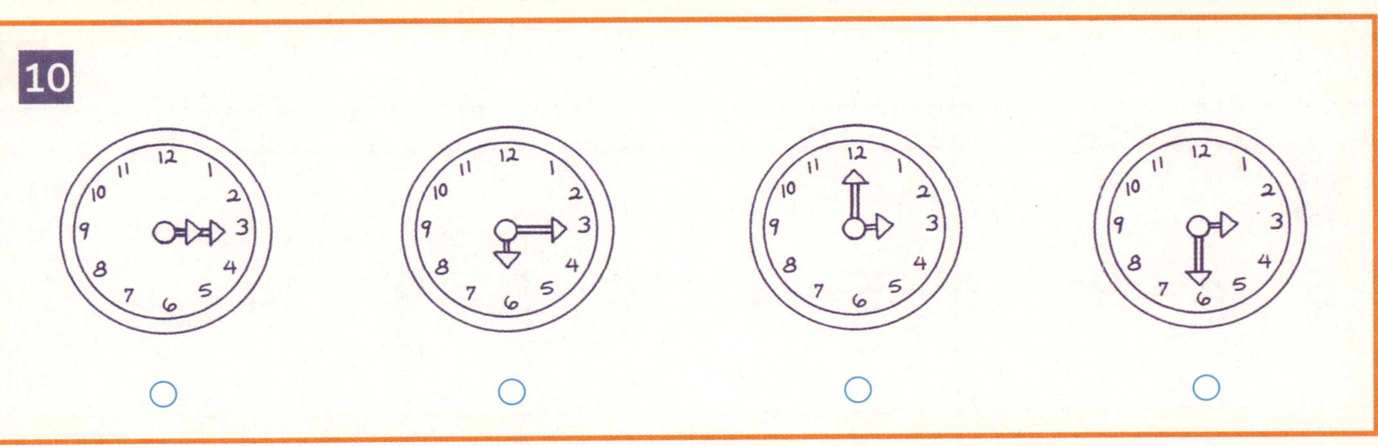

○ ○ ○ ○

11

44 ○ 52 ○ 59 ○ 61 ○

STOP

Test Yourself: Mathematics Problem Solving

SAMPLE

6309 ○ 639 ○ 693 ○ 60,039 ○

1

$5 + 4 = 9$ ○ $9 - 5 = 4$ ○ $4 + 5 = 9$ ○ $14 - 9 = 5$ ○

2

○

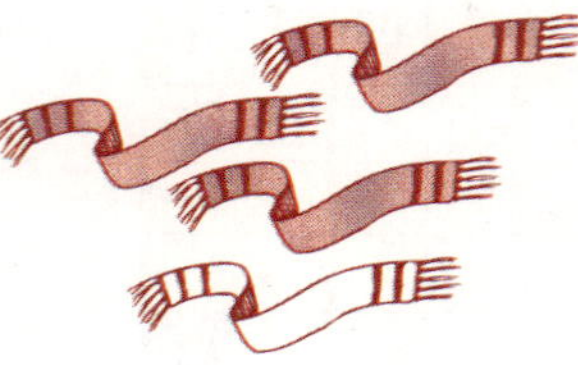
○

○

○

3

○

○

○

○

GO

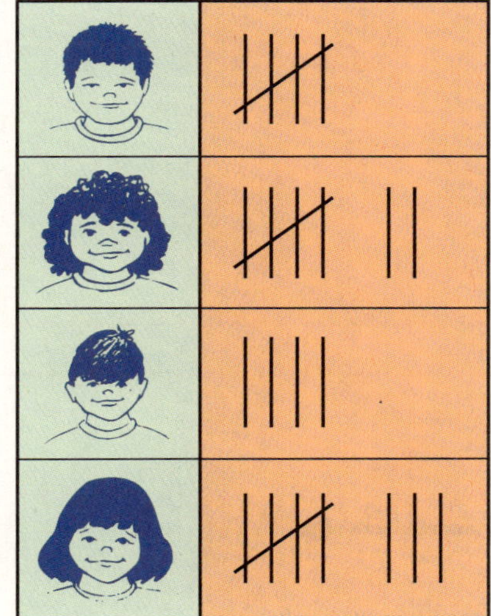

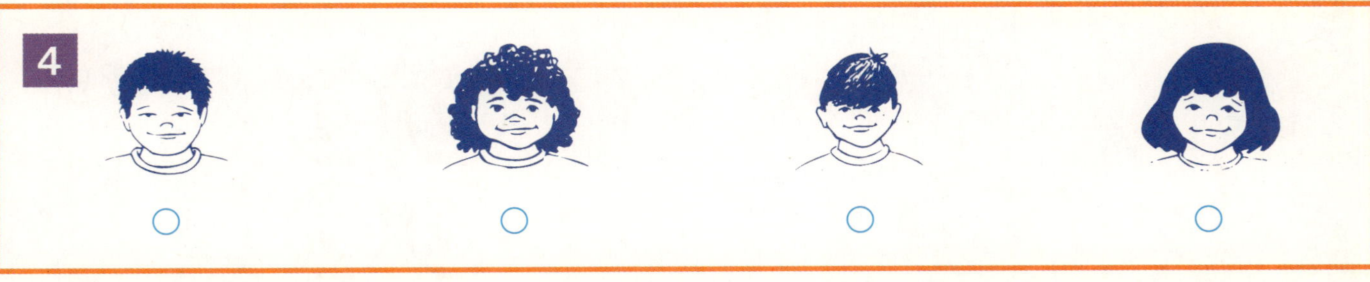

GO

7

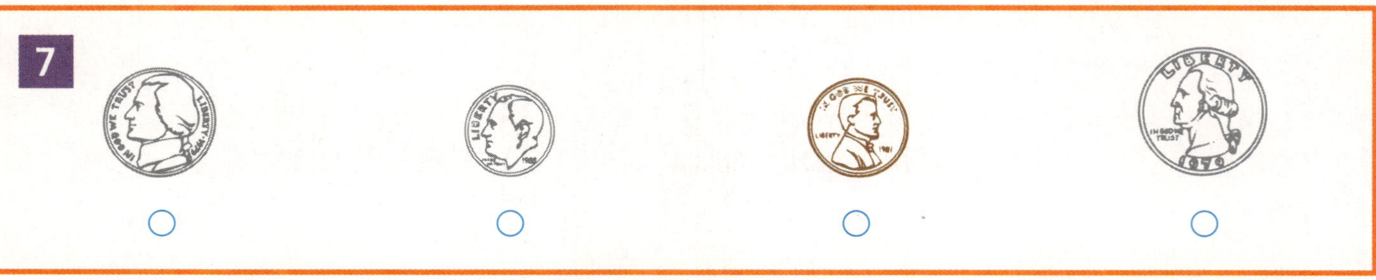

8

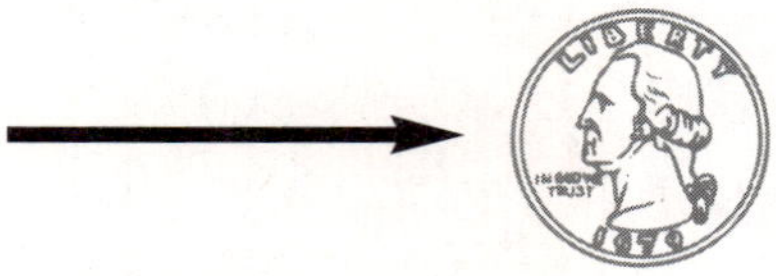

GO

9

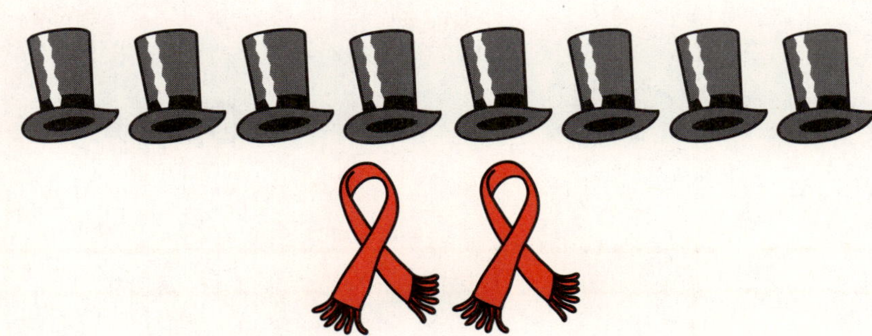

- ○ $10 - 2 = \square$
- ○ $2 + 8 = \square$
- ○ $6 + 2 = \square$
- ○ $8 - 2 = \square$

10

55	45	42	20
○	○	○	○

11

16	15	8	2
○	○	○	○

GO

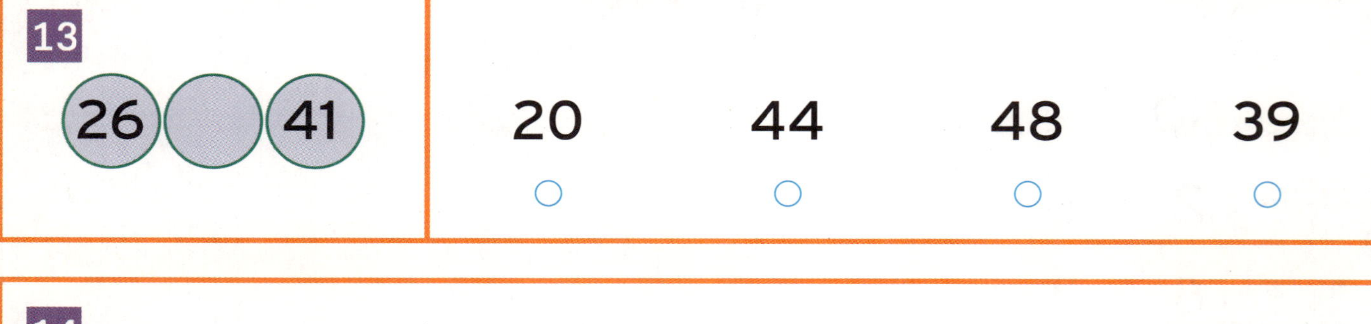

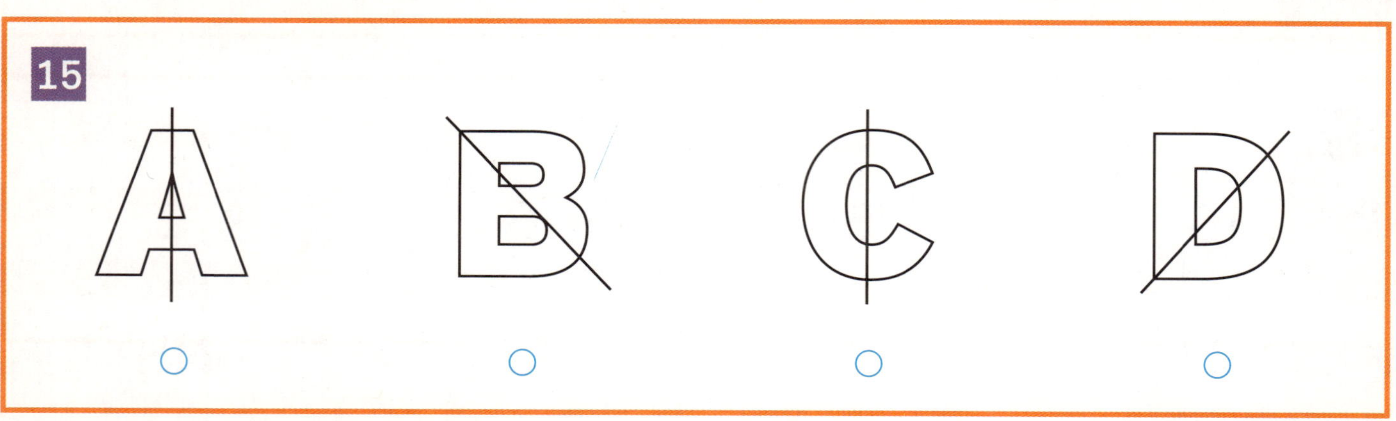

STOP

Unit 5

Mathematics Procedures

Lesson 6a Procedures

SAMPLE A

3

1

2 ○ 4 ○ 5 ○ NH ○

SAMPLE B

6 − 2 = □

1 ○ 3 ○ 6 ○ NH ○

Before you solve a problem, decide if you should add or subtract.

1

7 6

1 ○ 12 ○ 13 ○ NH ○

GO

2

$3 + 8 = \square$

5	10	11	NH
○	○	○	○

3

$$\begin{array}{r} 40 \\ +\ 50 \\ \hline \end{array}$$

45	90	100	NH
○	○	○	○

4

$12 - 2 = \square$

0	14	22	NH
○	○	○	○

STOP

Unit 5

Mathematics Procedures

Lesson 6b Procedures

Work carefully on scratch paper. Be sure to use the right numbers.

1

46

35

11 ○   13 ○   31 ○   NH ○

GO

2

$6 + 8 = \square$

14	16	18	NH
○	○	○	○

3

$$\begin{array}{r} 2 \\ 6 \\ +\ 3 \\ \hline \end{array}$$

8	11	15	NH
○	○	○	○

4

$$\begin{array}{r} 24 \\ -\ 3 \\ \hline \end{array}$$

14	21	27	NH
○	○	○	○

STOP

Unit 5

Test Yourself: Mathematics Procedures

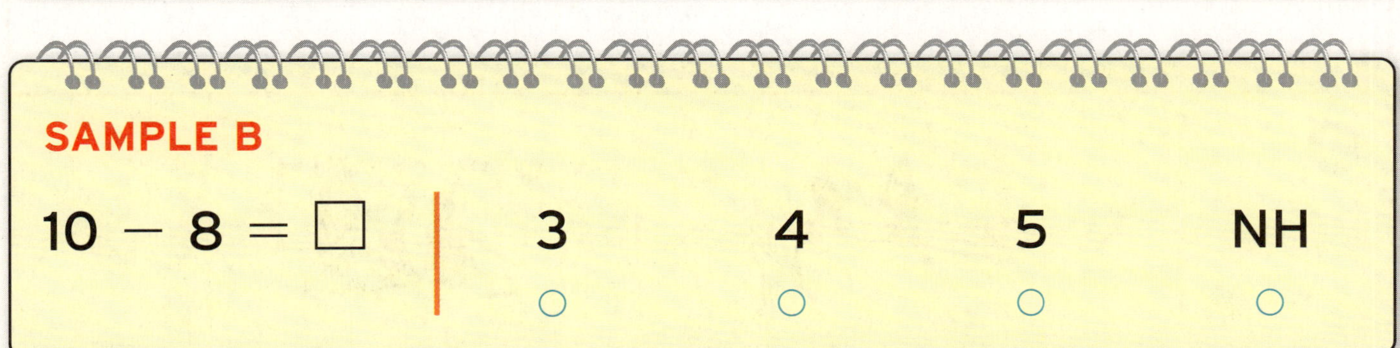

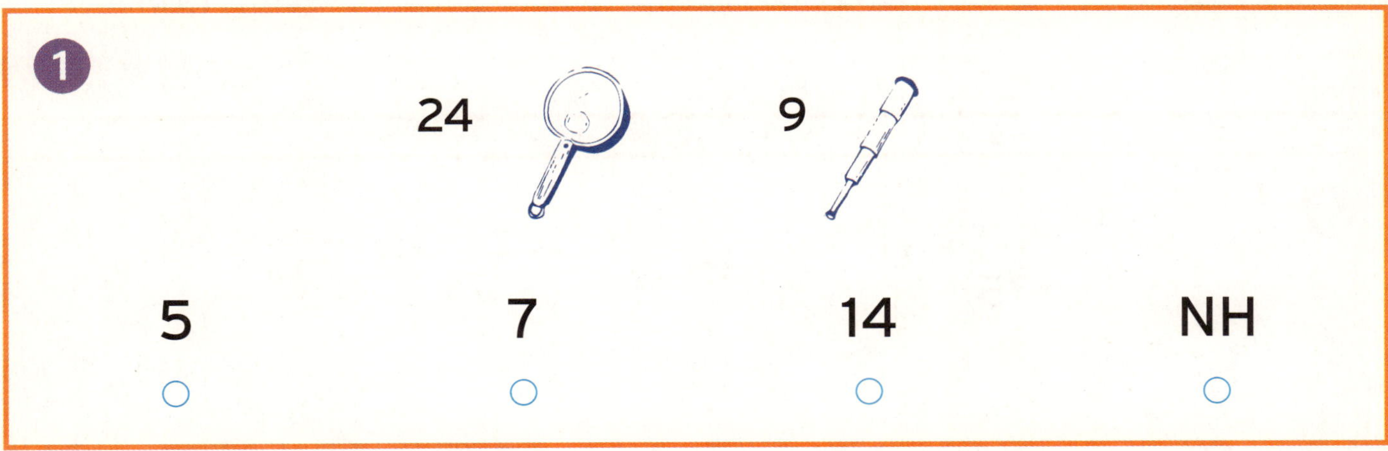

GO

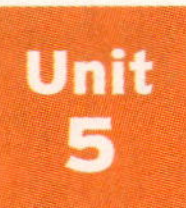

2

6 8

2 ○ 14 ○ 15 ○ NH ○

3

13 16

23 ○ 26 ○ 29 ○ NH ○

4

75 21

45 ○ 54 ○ 63 ○ NH ○

GO

5

$$\begin{array}{r} 70 \\ + \quad 9 \\ \hline \end{array}$$

79	97	709	NH
○	○	○	○

6

$$\begin{array}{r} 27 \\ + \quad 3 \\ \hline \end{array}$$

29	30	33	NH
○	○	○	○

7

$$\begin{array}{r} 65 \\ + \quad 81 \\ \hline \end{array}$$

136	144	145	NH
○	○	○	○

GO

8

$$\begin{array}{r} 200 \\ -\ 170 \\ \hline \end{array}$$

130	170	370	NH
○	○	○	○

9

$$\begin{array}{r} 918 \\ -\ 13 \\ \hline \end{array}$$

904	905	925	NH
○	○	○	○

10

$14 - 5 = \square$

9	10	19	NH
○	○	○	○

STOP

Unit 6

Spelling

Lesson 7a Spelling Skills

Look for the word that is spelled correctly.

1

wat ○ what ○ whut ○

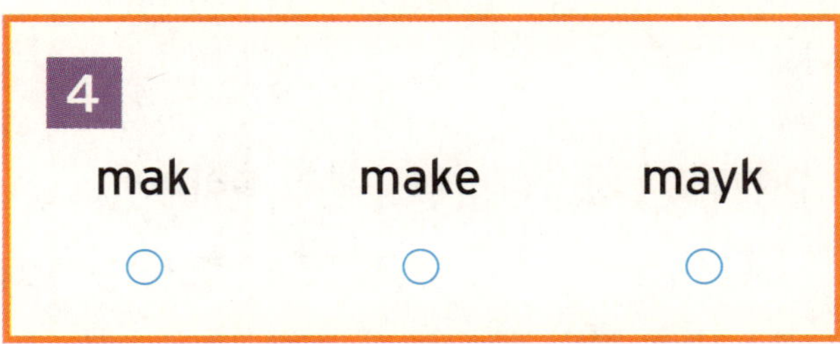

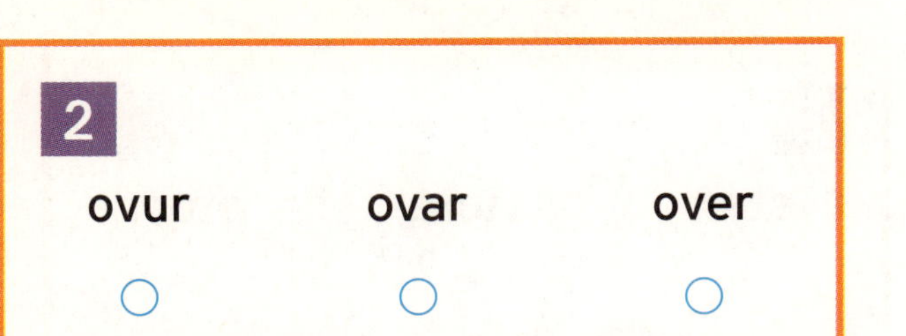

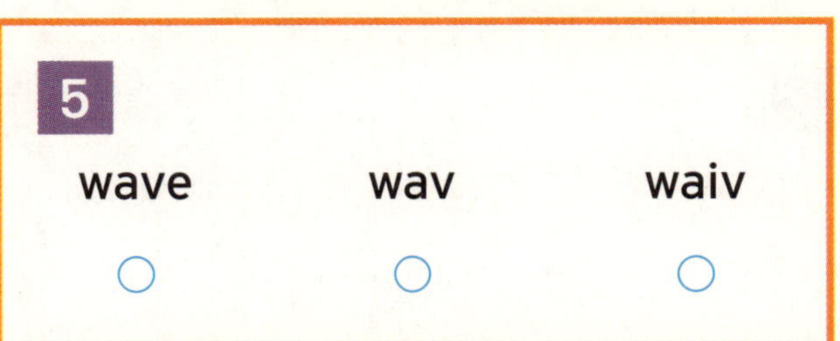

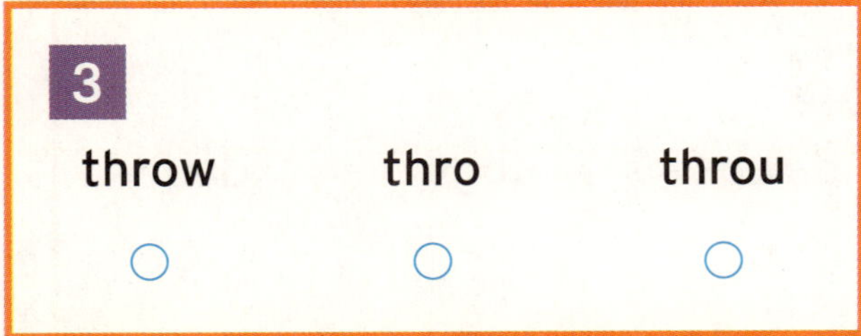

6

first ○ firzt ○ furst ○

STOP

Spelling

Lesson 7b Spelling Skills

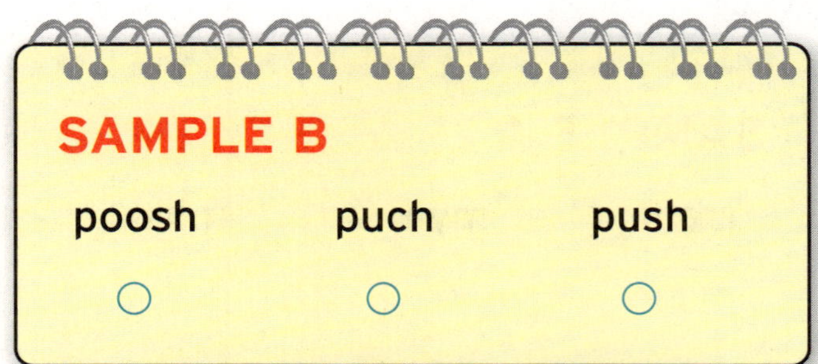

Look at each answer choice letter by letter for spelling mistakes. Then choose the answer that is spelled correctly.

1
paypr ○ paper ○ paiper ○

2
grau ○ grow ○ gro ○

3
unner ○ unter ○ under ○

4
safe ○ saif ○ saf ○

5
stor ○ store ○ stoor ○

6
dawgs ○ dogs ○ dogz ○

STOP

Unit 6

Test Yourself: Spelling

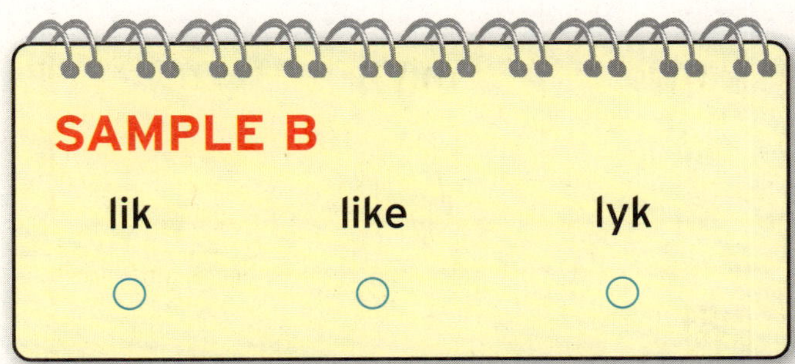

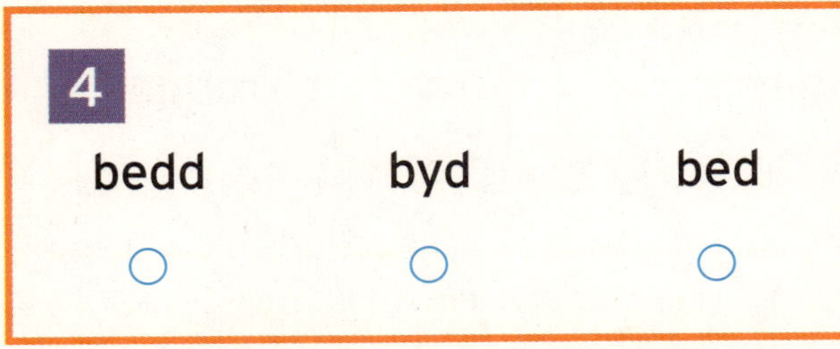

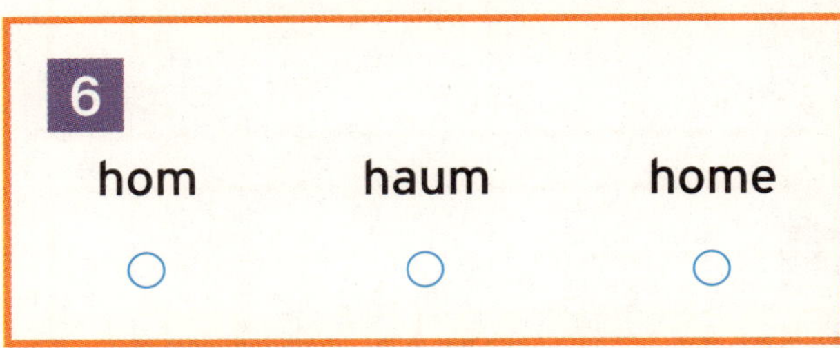

8

lion lian lyin

GO

9

mye ○ miy ○ my ○

10

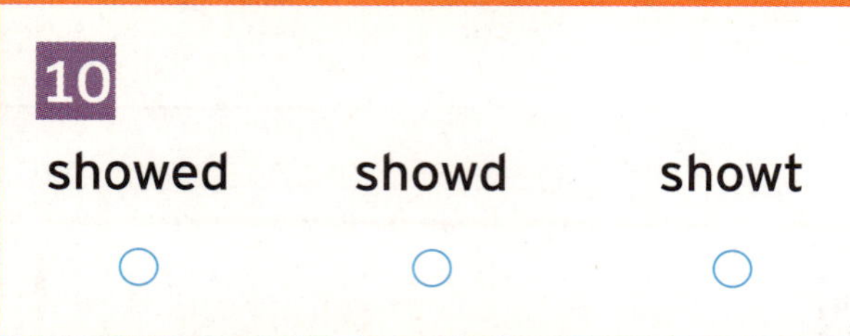

showed ○ showd ○ showt ○

11

tellng ○ teling ○ telling ○

12

learned ○ learnt ○ lernd ○

13

stoppeing ○ stoping ○ stopping ○

14

bushse ○ bushes ○ bushs ○

15

stayd ○ stade ○ stayed ○

STOP

Unit 7

Language

Lesson 8a Language Skills

SAMPLE A

mom carried the dishes to the table.

- ○ Mom carried
- ○ mom carry
- ○ The way it is

SAMPLE B

Yesterday we went to the park to play.

- ○ go
- ○ gone
- ○ The way it is

Look for mistakes in capitalization, punctuation, and word usage.

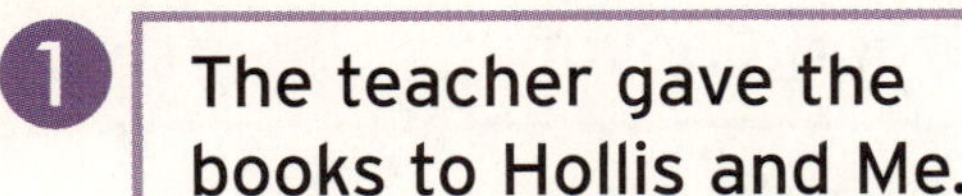

1. The teacher gave the books to Hollis and Me.

- ○ hollis and Me.
- ○ Hollis and me.
- ○ The way it is

2. Tynetta come to stay with us for a week.

- ○ came
- ○ coming
- ○ The way it is

3. Hey, Walter! Let's go swimming!

- ○ swimming.
- ○ swimming?
- ○ The way it is

4. Our Dad cook pancakes and eggs for breakfast.

- ○ cooked
- ○ cooking
- ○ The way it is

GO →

5 Her mother said the bowl had a goldfish in it?

- ○ it!
- ○ it.
- ○ The way it is

6 Our friend, Fatima, lives in Idaho.

- ○ Idaho?
- ○ idaho.
- ○ The way it is

7 The ball roll down the steps.

- ○ rolling
- ○ rolled
- ○ The way it is

8 The cat sat under the tree.

- ○ the Tree.
- ○ the tree?
- ○ The way it is

9 We saw elena at the soccer game.

- ○ seed Elena
- ○ saw Elena
- ○ The way it is

10 Last year we visit the Grand Canyon.

- ○ visited
- ○ visits
- ○ The way it is

GO

11. My friend used to live in Los angeles.

- ○ los angeles
- ○ Los Angeles
- ○ The way it is

12. Be careful, the plate is hot!

- ○ hot?
- ○ hot
- ○ The way it is

13. The book you want is on the desk.

- ○ desk?
- ○ Desk.
- ○ The way it is

14. Can we go to the swimming pool with you?

- ○ you
- ○ You?
- ○ The way it is

15. My sister catched the ball I threw.

- ○ caught
- ○ catching
- ○ The way it is

16. our school has a garden for butterflies.

- ○ our school have
- ○ Our school has
- ○ The way it is

GO →

Tim shaked the box to hear if it was empty.

- ○ shaking
- ○ shook
- ○ The way it is

18

My friend has a tent.

- ○ tent?
- ○ Tent!
- ○ The way it is

My teacher like to swim.

- ○ likes
- ○ liking
- ○ The way it is

STOP

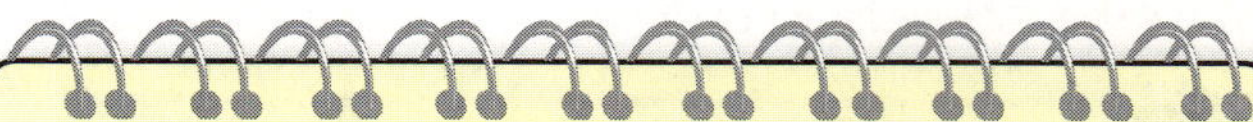

SAMPLE C

Nancy is writing a report about her town.

Which idea would go best at the beginning of her story?

- ○ The name of Nancy's school
- ○ How the town began
- ○ What sports Nancy plays

Toshi wants to write a story about a make-believe animal.

Which of these might he write about?

- ○ A neighbor's dog
- ○ A little kitten
- ○ A talking horse

STOP

Unit 7

Language

Lesson 8b Language Skills

SAMPLE A

The cow gave a loud moo. In the barn.

- ○ The cow gave a loud moo in the barn.
- ○ The cow. She gave a loud moo in the barn.
- ○ The way it is

SAMPLE B

Colorful leaves made the table pretty.

- ○ Colorful leaves. They made the table pretty.
- ○ Colorful leaves making the table pretty.
- ○ The way it is

Find the best way to write the sentence.

1 Our old cat never catching mice anymore.

- ○ Our old cat. She never catches mice anymore.
- ○ Our old cat never catches mice anymore.
- ○ The way it is

2 My sister is teaching me to play the piano.

- ○ My sister is teaching me. To play the piano.
- ○ My sister teach me to play the piano?
- ○ The way it is

STOP

SAMPLES

One day, Patrick and his big brother, Jeremy, went for a walk. They followed a path through some trees near their home. Suddenly, Jeremy stopped and pointed at something in front of them. Patrick looked and saw a baby rabbit sitting in the path.

SAMPLE C

Why was this story written?

- ○ To tell about what rabbits eat for food
- ○ To tell about two brothers going for a walk
- ○ To tell how to find baby rabbits in the woods

SAMPLE D

Which of these would go best after the last sentence?

- ○ It was much too hot for walking in the woods.
- ○ Rabbits hardly ever eat carrots.
- ○ They watched as the rabbit ate some clover.

Think about the story when you answer the questions.

Story 1

One day, my Dad and I started a leaf collection. We looked for leaves in our yard first. Then we went to the park and found lots more. Each leaf is a different shape. Dad showed me how to put the leaves in an old book to dry out.

3 Which of these would go best after the end of the last sentence?

- ○ My Dad likes to collect stamps and other things.
- ○ Then we pasted them in a scrapbook with their names.
- ○ After our walk, Dad decided he should take a nap.

4 Why was this story written?

- ○ To tell where to find lots of leaves
- ○ To tell about all different kinds of trees
- ○ To tell about making a leaf collection

GO

Story 2

Shakesia wanted to be a dancer. She saw dancers on television, but she had never seen them in person. Shakesia's parents decided to take her to see a real ballet in a theater! It was a secret. They told her they were going to see a movie.

 Why was this story written?

- ○ To tell about Shakesia's family
- ○ To tell about a surprise for Shakesia
- ○ To tell about a movie

 Which of these would <u>not</u> go with this story?

- ○ Shakesia was very surprised.
- ○ Shakesia practiced dancing often.
- ○ Shakesia has many friends.

STOP

Unit 7

Test Yourself: Language

SAMPLE A

Are you wearing your new shirt, Juan?

- ○ Juan.
- ○ Juan!
- ○ The way it is

SAMPLE B

Brad wrote to his friend in japan.

- ○ Japan.
- ○ japan?
- ○ The way it is

1 We took my cat to the vet on saturday.

- ○ Saturday?
- ○ Saturday.
- ○ The way it is

2 It rained while I was walking to school.

- ○ i was
- ○ I is
- ○ The way it is

3 Our uncle ride the bus to visit us.

- ○ rode
- ○ riding
- ○ The way it is

4 Wake up! You'll be late for school?

- ○ school!
- ○ School?
- ○ The way it is

GO

5 All her friends sent Mia cards when she was sick.

- ○ were sick.
- ○ was Sick.
- ○ The way it is

6 My brother yell when I go into his room.

- ○ yells
- ○ was yelling
- ○ The way it is

7 The store close at five o'clock.

- ○ be closing
- ○ closes
- ○ The way it is

8 Can you open this for me?

- ○ Me?
- ○ me.
- ○ The way it is

9 A girl named lucy just moved to our street.

- ○ named Lucy
- ○ names Lucy
- ○ The way it is

10 My family goes to the beach in New jersey.

- ○ new jersey.
- ○ New Jersey.
- ○ The way it is

STOP

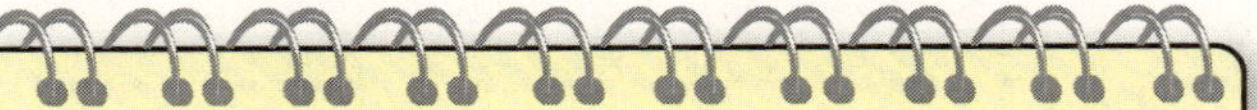

SAMPLE C

Our dog likes to sleep in the laundry.

- ○ Our dog likes to sleep. In the laundry.
- ○ Our dog. He likes to sleep in the laundry.
- ● The way it is

11 My brother Roberto. He knows how to ride a bike.

- ● My brother Roberto knows how to ride a bike.
- ○ My brother Roberto knowing how to ride a bike.
- ○ The way it is

12 Dad came home. Late for dinner.

- ○ Dad coming home late for dinner.
- ● Dad came home late for dinner.
- ○ The way it is

13 Dan is playing with his toy truck in the yard.

- ○ Dan plays with his toy truck. In the yard.
- ○ Dan. He plays with his toy truck in the yard.
- ● The way it is

GO

I am reading. The book on the table.

- I am reading the book on the table.
- I am reading the book. On the table
- The way it is

This morning I left my gloves at home.

- This morning I left. My gloves at home.
- This morning. I left my gloves at home.
- The way it is

The cat sat beside. The sunny window.

- The cat sat. Beside the sunny window.
- The cat sat beside the sunny window.
- The way it is

The driver wanting to park the car.

- The driver wanted to park the car.
- The driver want. To park the car.
- The way it is

STOP

SAMPLES

My Mom and Dad took me fishing at the lake. I didn't want to touch worms, so I used marshmallows instead. Guess who caught a fish! My Dad didn't. My Mom didn't. I caught a big, shiny fish with a red marshmallow!

SAMPLE D

Which of these would go best after the last sentence?

- ○ Mom and Dad asked if they could use a marshmallow.
- ○ Sometimes, we even toast big marshmallows on a campfire.
- ○ We go fishing in the lake that is in our city park.

SAMPLE E

Why was this story written?

- ○ To teach you how to fish
- ○ To make you laugh
- ○ To make you want to go fishing

GO

Story 1

Last summer my family went to visit our cousins on a farm. I saw so many different animals! There were cows, horses, goats, and chickens. The best ones were wild animals. One night, we saw three deer in the field. They were so beautiful in the moonlight.

18 Which of these would not go with this story?

- ○ My cousins are a year older and a year younger than me.
- ○ My cousins have to ride the bus to go to school.
- ○ One day, we took turns riding one of the horses.

19 Why was this story written?

- ○ To tell about a trip to a farm
- ○ To explain how to raise animals
- ○ To make you laugh

GO

Story 2

Jared and his sister, Suelee, took a walk in the woods. Their Uncle Walter went along, too. They saw a squirrel and lots of different birds. Jared even found a big turtle under a log.

20. Which of these would not go with this story?

- ○ Suelee liked to find pinecones for her nature collection.
- ○ Jared liked the woods even more than playing sports.
- ○ Jared's uncle drove a really big truck with a loud horn.

21. Which of these would go best after the last sentence?

- ○ There are different kinds of squirrels.
- ○ Uncle Walter writes books for children.
- ○ They looked at the turtle but didn't touch it.

GO

Story 3

Here is how to make my favorite treat. Peel a banana. Don't eat it yet. Put a little peanut butter on the banana. Then take a bite. It's delicious.

22 Why was this story written?

- ● To explain how to make a treat
- ○ To tell a joke about bananas
- ○ To show how to cook something

23 Which of these would go best after the last sentence?

- ○ You should not eat too many treats.
- ○ Bananas come from warm countries.
- ● This treat is also good for you.

24 Which of these does not go with this story?

- ● Making this treat is very simple.
- ○ Bananas grow in warm places.
- ○ You can use any kind of peanut butter.

STOP

Listening

Lesson 9a Listening Skills

SAMPLE A

- ○ leaf
- ○ snow
- ○ stone

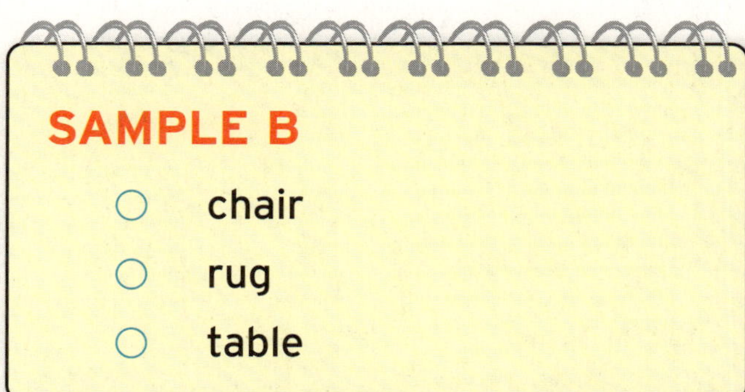

SAMPLE B

- ○ chair
- ○ rug
- ○ table

Listen carefully while you look at the words or pictures.

1

- ○ cold
- ○ wet
- ○ level

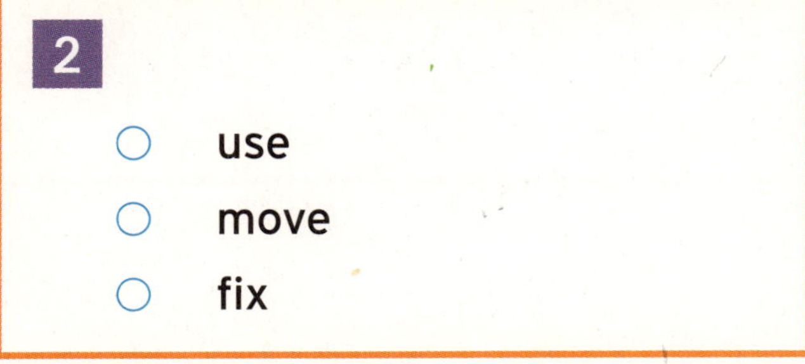

2

- ○ use
- ○ move
- ○ fix

3

- ○ freeze
- ○ crack
- ○ melt

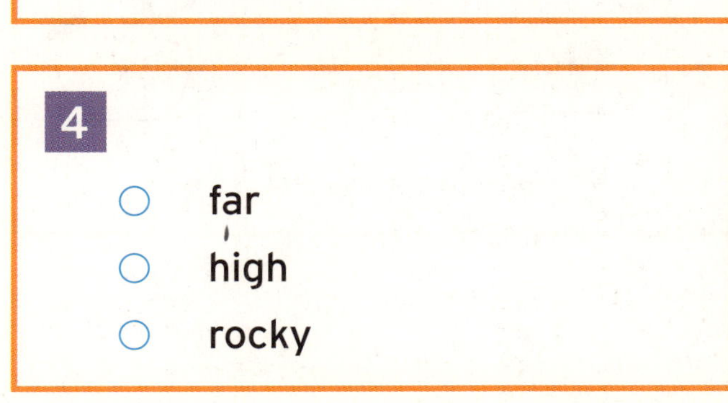

4

- ○ far
- ○ high
- ○ rocky

GO →

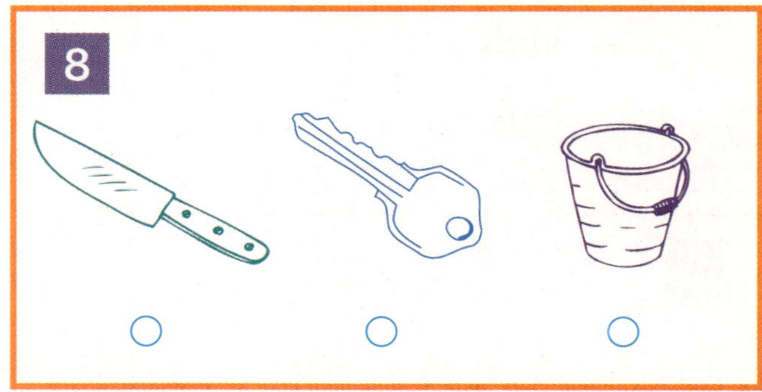

STOP

Listening

Lesson 9b Listening Skills

SAMPLE A

- ○ in the library
- ○ on the school lawn
- ○ in the gymnasium

SAMPLE B

- ○ afternoon
- ○ night
- ○ morning

If you aren't sure which answer is correct, take your best guess.

1

- ○ shop
- ○ walk
- ○ eat

2

- ○ shopping in a mall
- ○ why children like a mall
- ○ an unusual use for a mall

3

- ○ To have her eyes tested
- ○ To have her ears tested
- ○ Because she had a cold

4

- ○ petted the dog
- ○ saw the dog
- ○ talked to the doctor

GO

5

- ○ In a tree
- ○ Near the garden
- ○ Under the feeder

6

- ○ His mother
- ○ His sister
- ○ His father

7

- ○ Pigeons
- ○ Quail
- ○ Geese

8

- ○ Cotton-top
- ○ Long-legs
- ○ Band-tail

9

- ○ River Animals
- ○ All About Crawfish
- ○ Not A Fish

10

- ○ Lobster
- ○ Shark
- ○ Frog

11

- ○ Chasing after other fish
- ○ Making noise
- ○ Hiding from other fish

12

- ○ Flatfish
- ○ Crayfish
- ○ Crawdad

STOP

Unit 8

Test Yourself: Listening

SAMPLE A

- ○ solved
- ○ avoided
- ● found

SAMPLE B

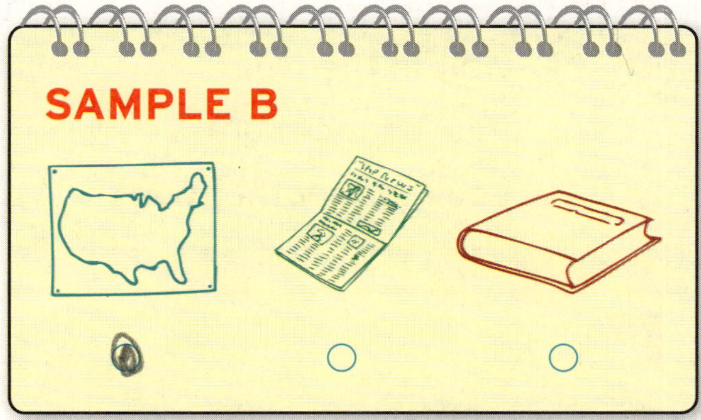

1

- ○ end
- ● beginning
- ○ bottom

2

- ○ worried
- ○ happy
- ● unaware

3

4

GO

SAMPLE C

- ○ Wait in the tree
- ● Pick up more grass
- ○ Look for another bug

5

- ○ waffles
- ○ jelly
- ● bread

6

- ● "A Mexican Treat"
- ○ "Better Than Bread"
- ○ "A Different Kind of Food"

7

- ○ baked tortilla
- ● cheese crisp
- ○ tortilla snack

8

- ● wheat or corn flour
- ○ only wheat flour
- ○ only corn flour

9

- ○ In the river
- ○ Near a cave
- ● Under a tree

10

- ○ He was sleeping.
- ● He had a cool and shady spot.
- ○ He had a book with him.

11

- ● An owl
- ○ A duck
- ○ A butterfly

12

- ○ Go swimming
- ○ Explore the forest
- ● Meet the other animals

GO

13

- It was tall
- It had pinecones
- It had flowers

14

- On the sidewalk
- On the grass
- On a tree

15

- Walk to the park
- Walk to the store
- Walk to the school

16

- Ride in the wagon
- Look for pinecones
- Climb a tree

17

- A new store
- A new flower
- A new tree

18

- Wash the dishes
- Make the beds
- Plan the trip

19

- In the bedroom
- In the living room
- In the camper

20

- Bird
- Rock
- Hook

21

- careful
- silly
- friendly

GO

22

- ○ Notepaper
- ○ Paper towels
- ○ Some pens

23

- ○ hold the ink
- ○ cut the stamp
- ○ wash the potato

24

- ○ Cut out a design
- ○ Dip the stamp in ink
- ○ Get a clean towel

25

- ○ It is used to mail letters.
- ○ It gets stepped on.
- ○ It leaves a mark.

26

- ○ Making it cool
- ○ Covering it up
- ○ Keeping it flat

27

- ○ Nails would make tires flat
- ○ Nails would make the roof leak
- ○ Nails would be reused

28

- ○ How to build a wood cabin
- ○ How to make a dirt road
- ○ How to use an old roof

STOP

Unit 9

Test Practice

Test 1 Word Study Skills

SAMPLE A

- ○ monkey
- ○ eggshell
- ○ ladder

SAMPLE B

- ○ cleaned
- ○ cleans
- ○ cleaning

1

- ○ opening
- ○ candle
- ○ anybody

2

- ○ morning
- ○ snowball
- ○ kitchen

3

- ○ chicken
- ○ borrow
- ○ mailbox

STOP 

- ○ mixed
- ○ mixes
- ○ mixing

- ○ softly
- ○ softest
- ○ softer

- ○ dropping
- ○ drops
- ○ dropped

STOP 

SAMPLE C

don't didn't doesn't

7 we'll we've we're

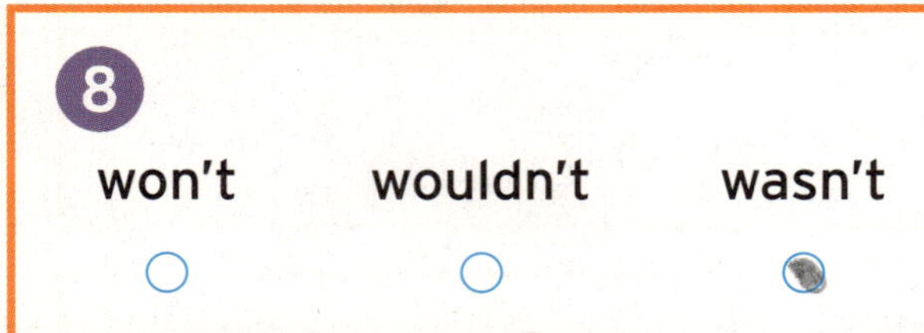

8 won't wouldn't wasn't

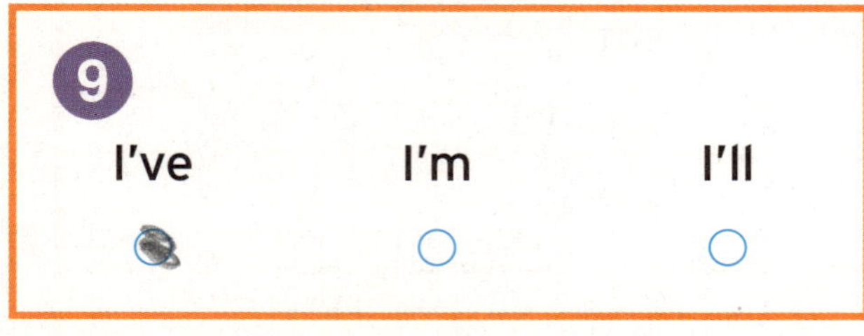

9 I've I'm I'll

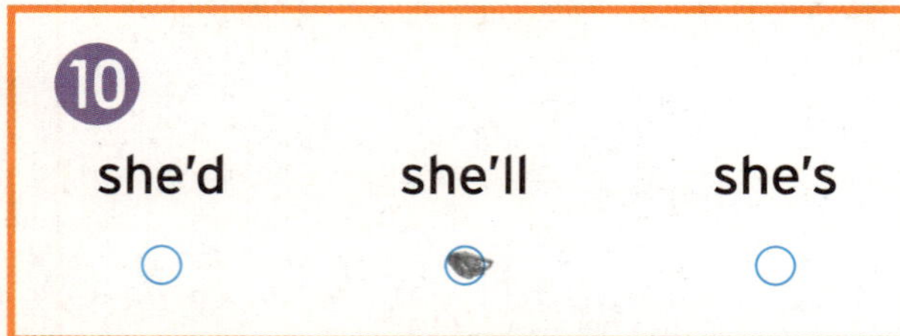

10 she'd she'll she's

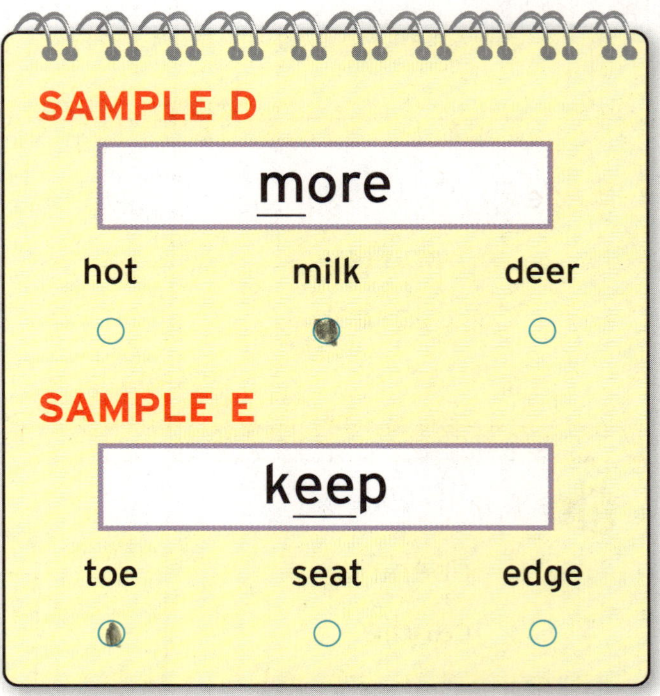

SAMPLE D

more

hot milk deer

SAMPLE E

keep

toe seat edge

11 dish

pile need love

12 burn

learn run group

STOP

GO

13
clock
knee
look
city

14
fast
plate
grab
air

15
shout
four
new
how

16
think
what
tell
path

17
sleep
slow
small
lost

18
draw
drink
dark
mow

19
buy
blue
heavy
pie

20
park
phone
jump
care

21
happy
eat
why
make

22
game
meat
hands
train

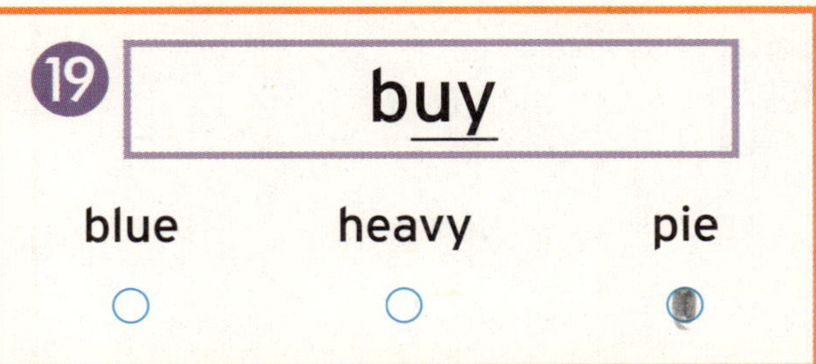

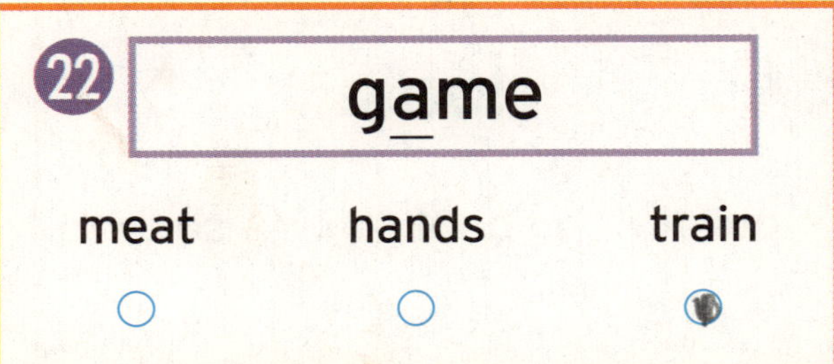

GO

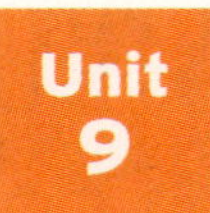
Unit
9

23
much
fun
child
kitten

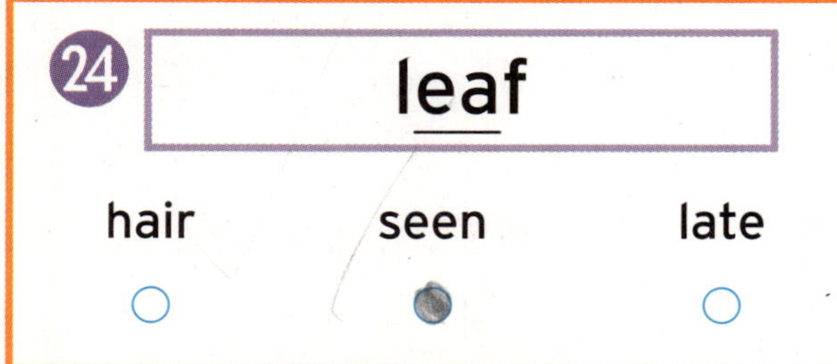
24
leaf
hair
seen
late

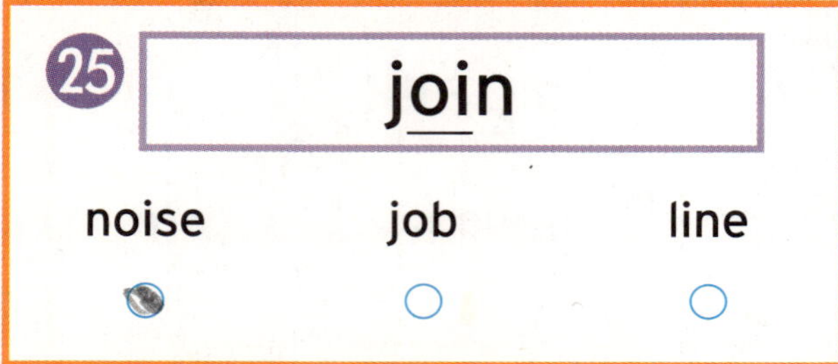
25
join
noise
job
line

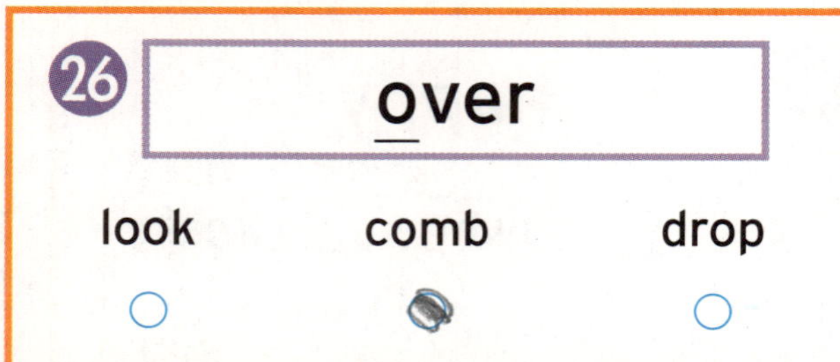
26
over
look
comb
drop

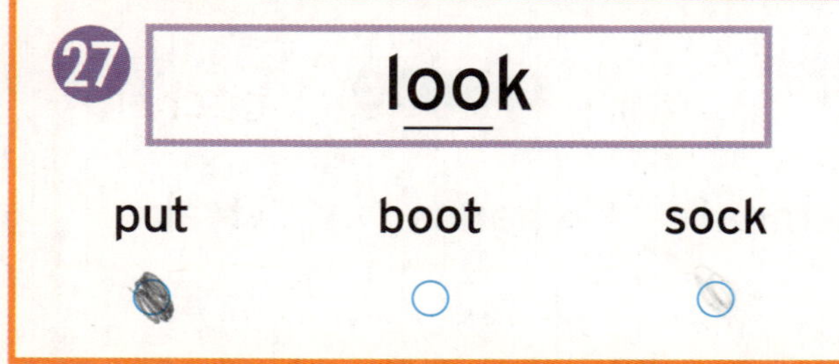
27
look
put
boot
sock

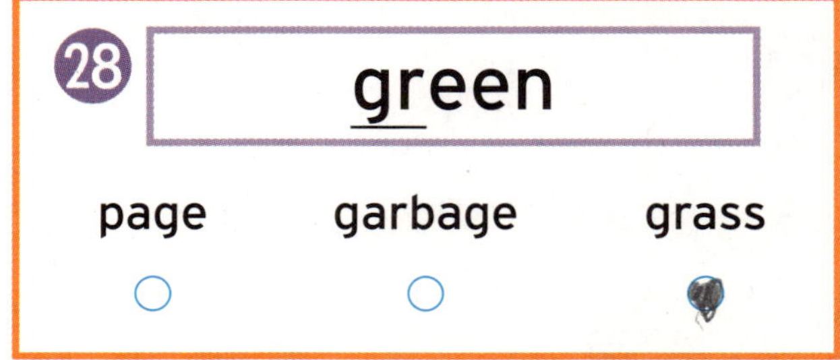
28
green
page
garbage
grass

29
light
chair
mine
finish

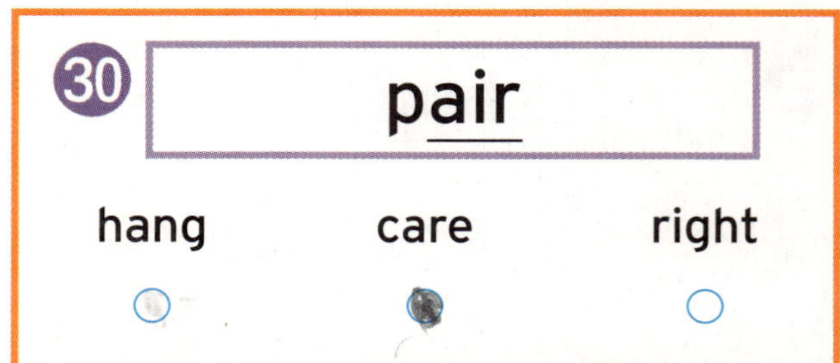
30
pair
hang
care
right

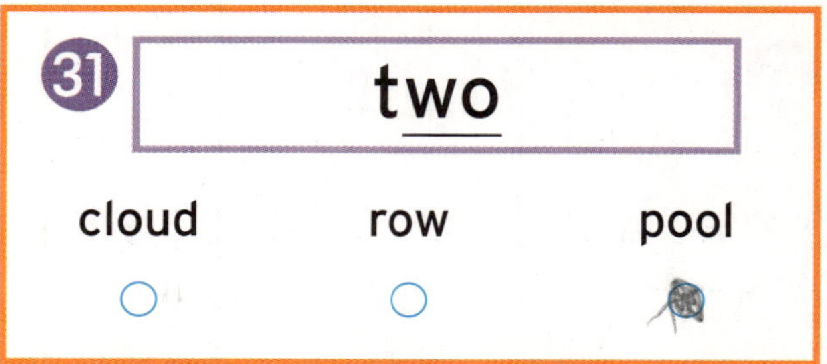
31
two
cloud
row
pool

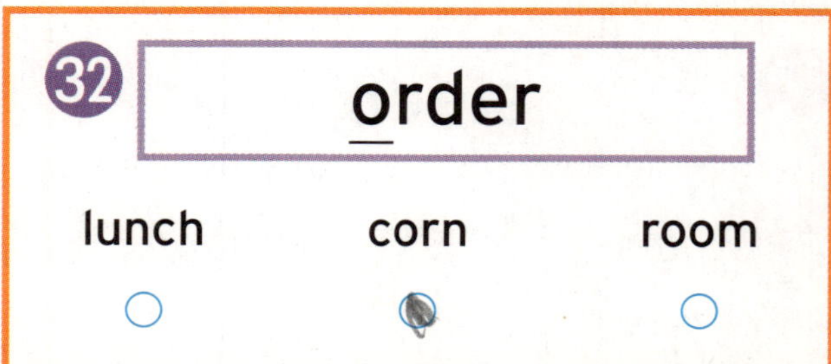
32
order
lunch
corn
room

STOP

Unit 9

Test Practice

Test 2 Word Reading

SAMPLE

A	hungry ○	plans ○	flowers ●
B	bear ○	floor ○	garden ○
C	bees ○	fire ○	hide ○

1–3

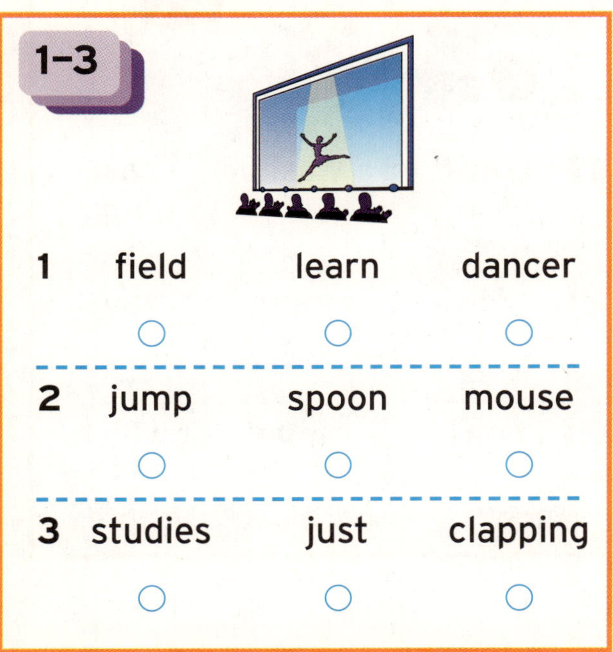

1	field ○	learn ○	dancer ○
2	jump ○	spoon ○	mouse ○
3	studies ○	just ○	clapping ○

4–6

4	walking ○	finds ○	children ○
5	rope ○	part ○	weigh ○
6	rode ○	waiting ○	hot ○

7–9

7	window ○	quit ○	tried ○
8	cat ○	windy ○	slip ○
9	pat ○	sleep ○	kitchen ○

GO

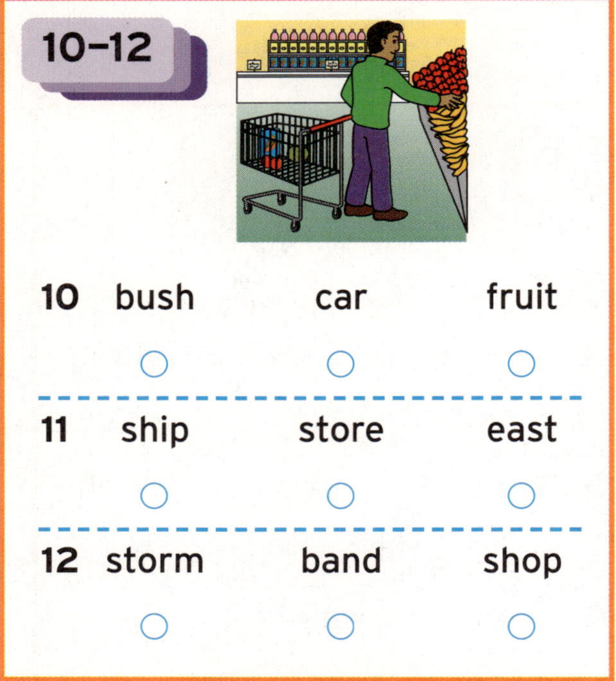

10–12

10	bush	car	fruit
11	ship	store	east
12	storm	band	shop

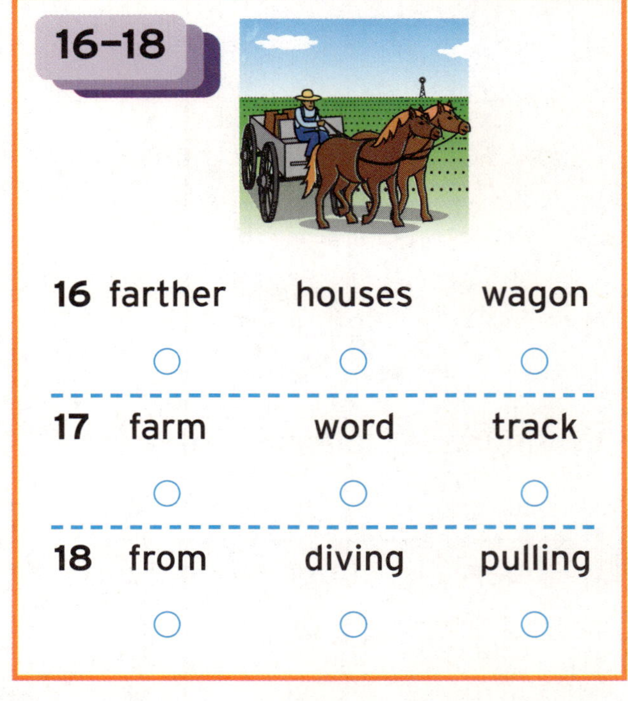

16–18

16	farther	houses	wagon
17	farm	word	track
18	from	diving	pulling

13–15

13	balloon	scold	forest
14	three	snow	bill
15	cold	went	soon

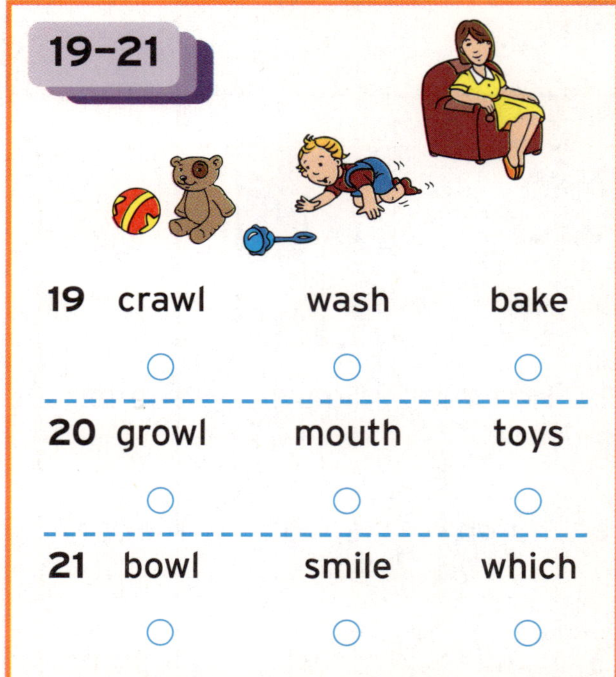

19–21

19	crawl	wash	bake
20	growl	mouth	toys
21	bowl	smile	which

Unit 9 Test Practice

Test 3 Reading Comprehension

The tree has lots of apples.

He tied string around the papers.

SAMPLE B

The frog is jumping.

3

The family is in the kitchen.

4

It is cold. Marta is going outside.

STOP

SAMPLE C

You use it to eat.

It is sharp.

5

It helps keep you dry.

It goes on your head.

6

It is large.

It eats grass.

7

It likes to swim.

It lays eggs.

8

It helps plants grow.

It gives light.

9

You can ride it.

It has wheels.

STOP

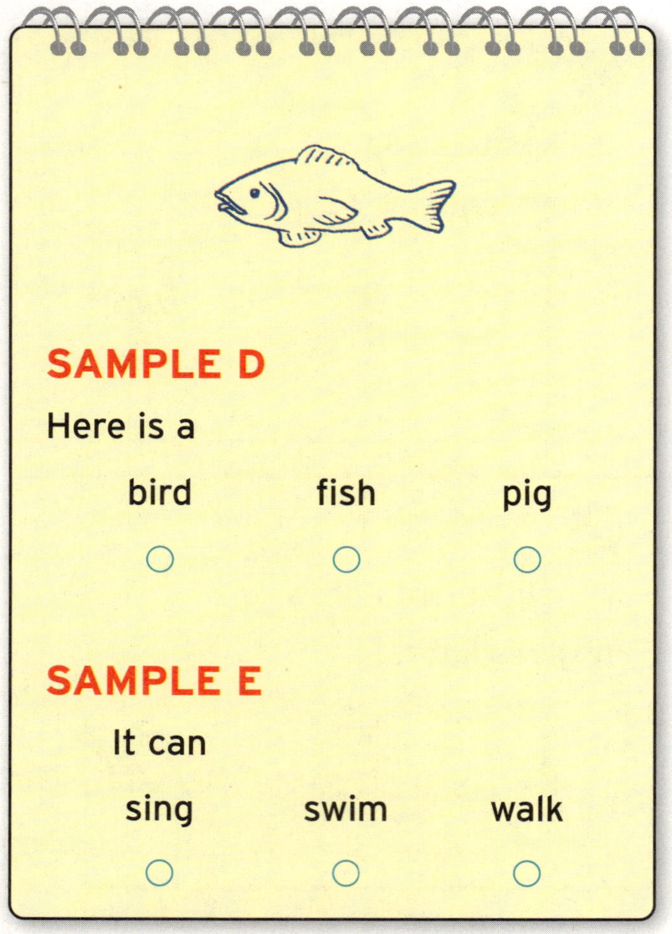

SAMPLE D

Here is a

bird fish pig

○ ○ ○

SAMPLE E

It can

sing swim walk

○ ○ ○

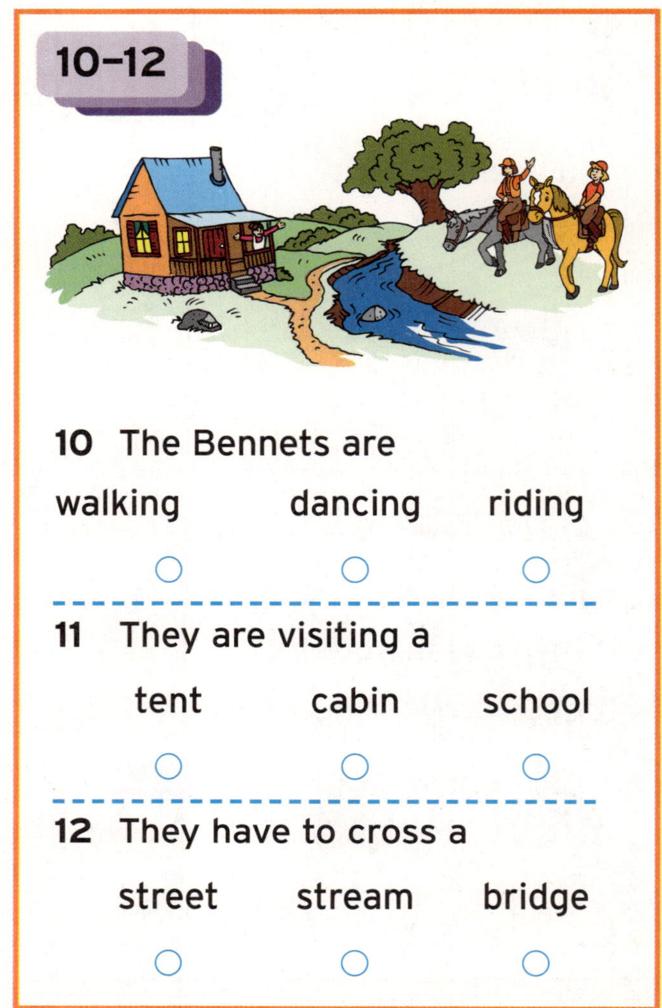

10–12

10 The Bennets are

walking dancing riding

○ ○ ○

11 They are visiting a

tent cabin school

○ ○ ○

12 They have to cross a

street stream bridge

○ ○ ○

STOP

SAMPLES

Whales

Whales live in the ocean. They have fins and tails, and they are good swimmers. Whales look like fish, but they are not fish. Whales have smooth skin instead of scales. Whales cannot breathe underwater like fish. They breathe air, just like people.

SAMPLE F

This story tells some ways that whales

- ○ are different from fish
- ○ find each other
- ○ learn to swim

SAMPLE G

Whales do not have

- ○ fins
- ○ tails
- ○ scales

GO

Jamila's Chalk

Jamila has a box of chalk. She draws pretty pictures in front of her house. Jamila helps her baby brother make pictures, too. When Sara visits, Jamila and Sara draw animals. Jamila likes having chalk.

13. Jamila helps her brother
    - ○ jump
    - ○ draw
    - ○ talk

14. This story tells how Jamila
    - ○ asked for her chalk
    - ○ uses her chalk
    - ○ finds her chalk

15. Jamila and Sara like to draw
    - ○ animals
    - ○ flowers
    - ○ cars

16. You can tell Jamila feels
    - ○ lonely
    - ○ sad
    - ○ happy

GO →

Hidden Toys

Kenny took his favorite toys and hid them in the basement. He asked his friends to come and find them. Then he made a sign.

> Take two steps from the door.
> Turn right. Take five steps.
> Follow the stairs. Stand under the light.
> Turn left. Take three steps.
> Open the door. Enjoy the secret!

17 Where did Kenny hide his toys?

- ○ At his school
- ○ In his yard
- ○ In his house

18 What does Kenny's sign tell?

- ○ Why Kenny hid his toys
- ○ Where Kenny's house is
- ○ Where the toys are hidden

19 Why did Kenny hide his toys?

- ○ He wanted his friends to find them.
- ○ He wanted to keep them for himself.
- ○ They were old and broken.

Duck and Owl

"How nice it will be to play with Owl," Duck said to herself. "We can have a picnic." Duck floated past Frog's log.

"Hello, Duck," he croaked. "I thought you were playing with Owl today."

"I am waiting for him to come to the pond," answered Duck.

Frog laughed. "Owl is waiting in the woods. He thinks you are playing in his tree today."

"How did we get so mixed up?" asked Duck.

"Come with me," said Frog. "I will show you where Owl's tree is."

20 Where was Duck waiting for Owl?

- ○ In the water
- ○ In the woods
- ○ In her nest

21 What was Duck planning for Owl?

- ○ A game
- ○ A picnic
- ○ A party

22 Frog and Duck went together to

- ○ Frog's log
- ○ Duck's pond
- ○ Owl's tree

Kelly's Soccer Game

My name is Kelly. On Saturday, my dad will take me to my first soccer game. My coach wrote down how to get there. This is what the coach's note said:

1. Go down Oak Street. Go across the bridge.
2. Turn left onto Stark Street. Go five blocks.
3. Turn right onto Front Street. Stop at Clark School.
   The field is behind the school.

23 The soccer field is on

- ○ Stark Street
- ○ Oak Street
- ○ Front Street

24 At the bridge, Kelly's dad should

- ○ go straight
- ○ turn right
- ○ park the car

GO →

Hot-Air Balloons

It is fun to fly a hot-air balloon. A big fan blows air into the balloon. The balloon must be full of hot air to make it fly. Next, the pilot checks the ropes. The ropes hold the basket under the balloon. The pilot climbs into the basket. A helper frees the balloon from the ground. Slowly, the balloon rises into the air.

25. The first step is to

- ○ check the basket
- ○ untie the ropes
- ○ fill the balloon

26. In this story, a basket is used to

- ○ hold the fan
- ○ carry the pilot
- ○ heat the air

27. What makes the balloon fly?

- ○ A big fan
- ○ Hot air
- ○ Ropes

STOP

Unit 9

Test Practice

Test 4 **Mathematics Problem Solving**

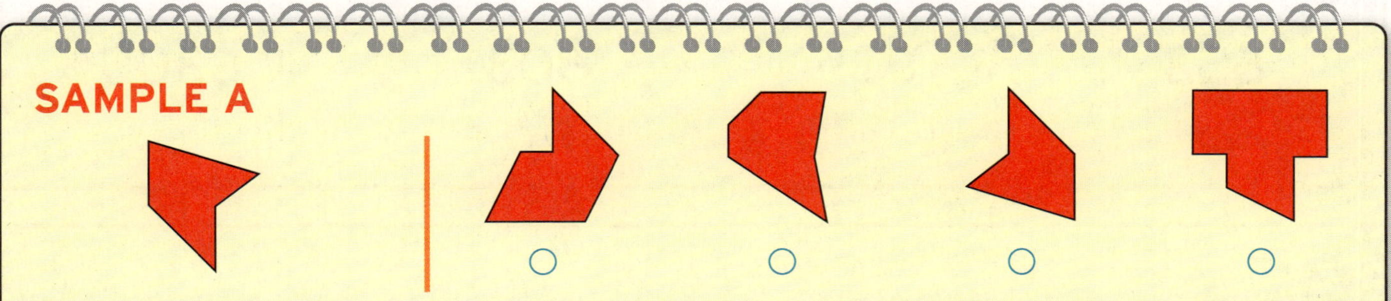

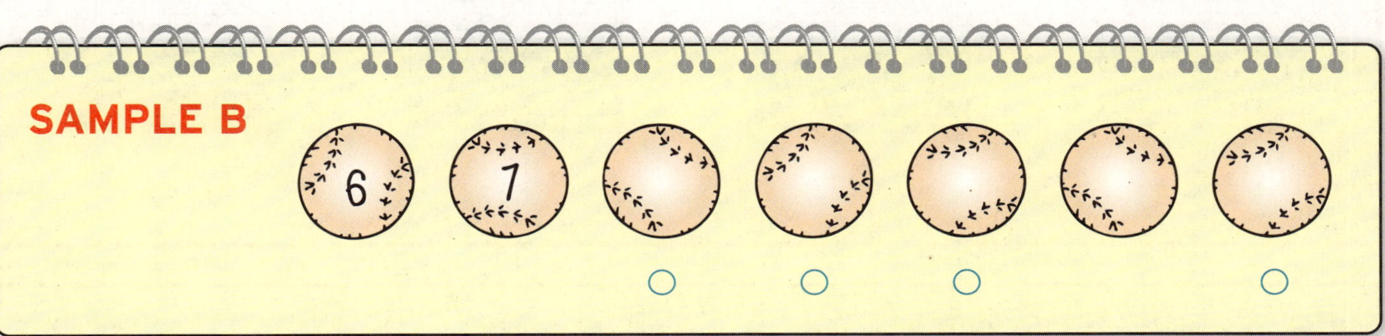

34 ○ | 35 ○ | 36 ○ | 37 ○

2

87 ○ | 780 ○ | 78 ○ | 708 ○

GO

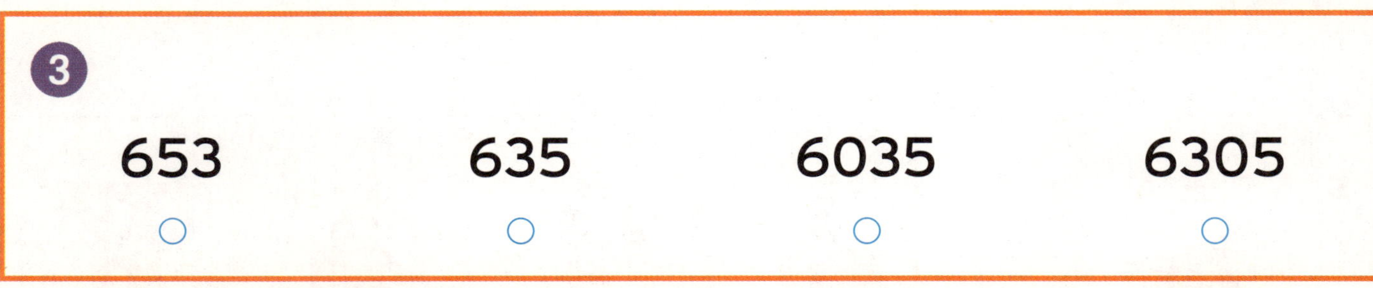

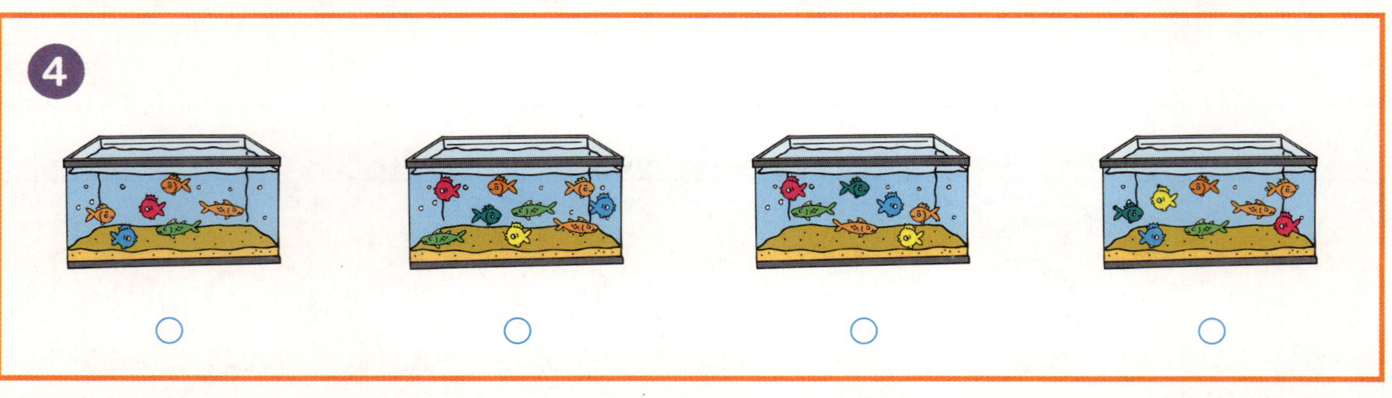

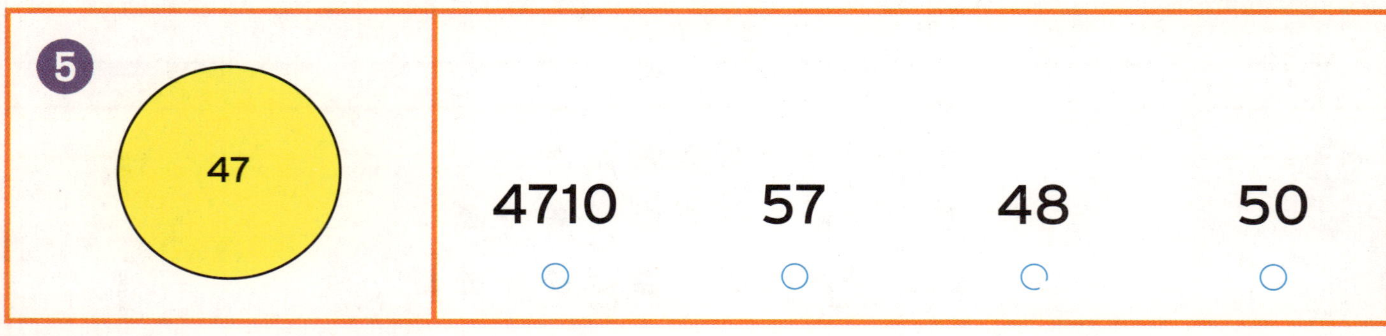

GO

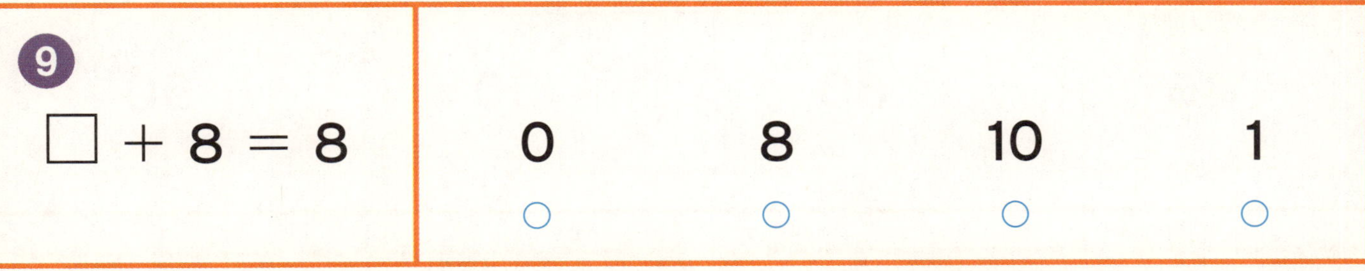

9

□ + 8 = 8

0 8 10 1

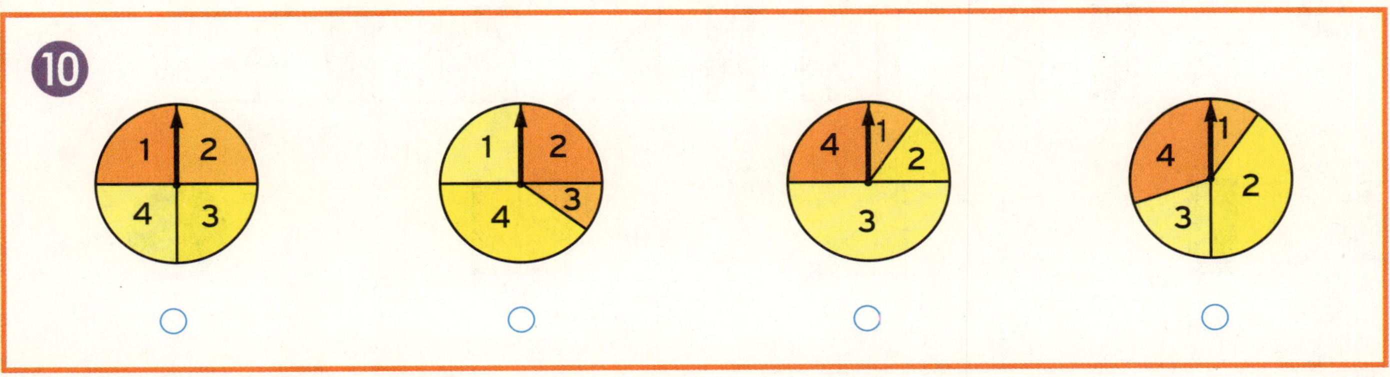

GO

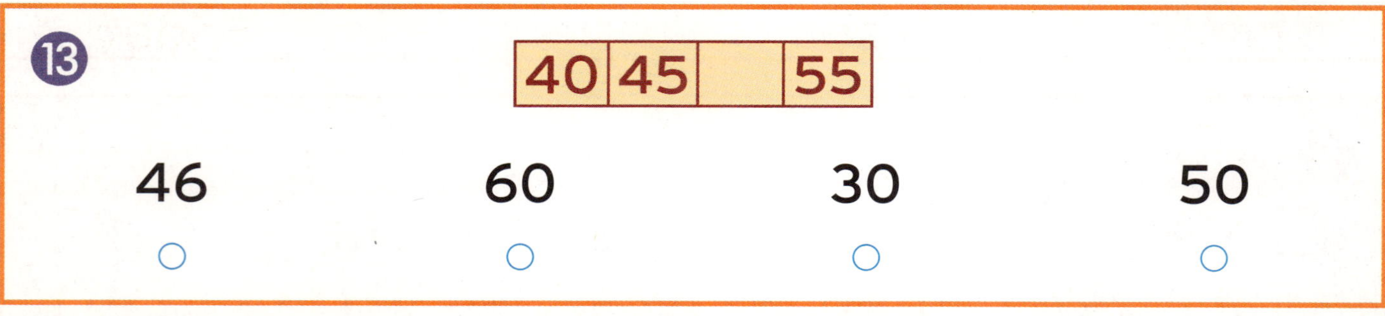

GO

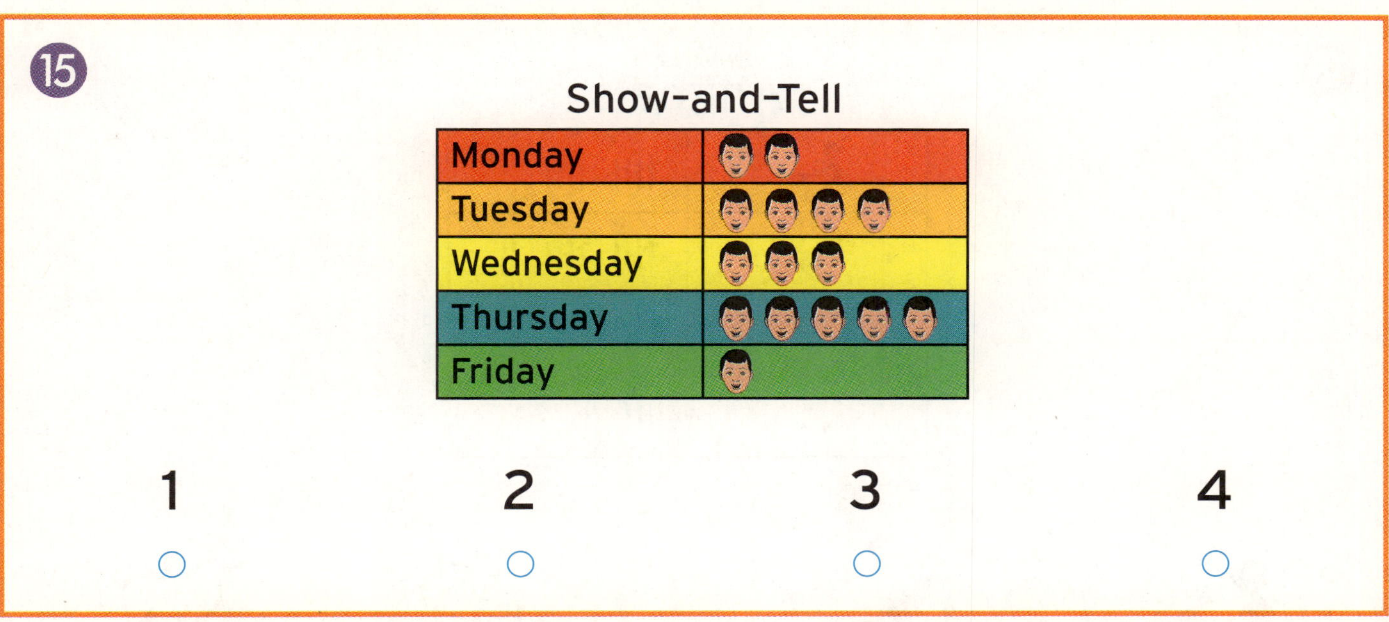

15

Show-and-Tell

Monday	2 faces
Tuesday	4 faces
Wednesday	3 faces
Thursday	5 faces
Friday	1 face

1 ○ 2 ○ 3 ○ 4 ○

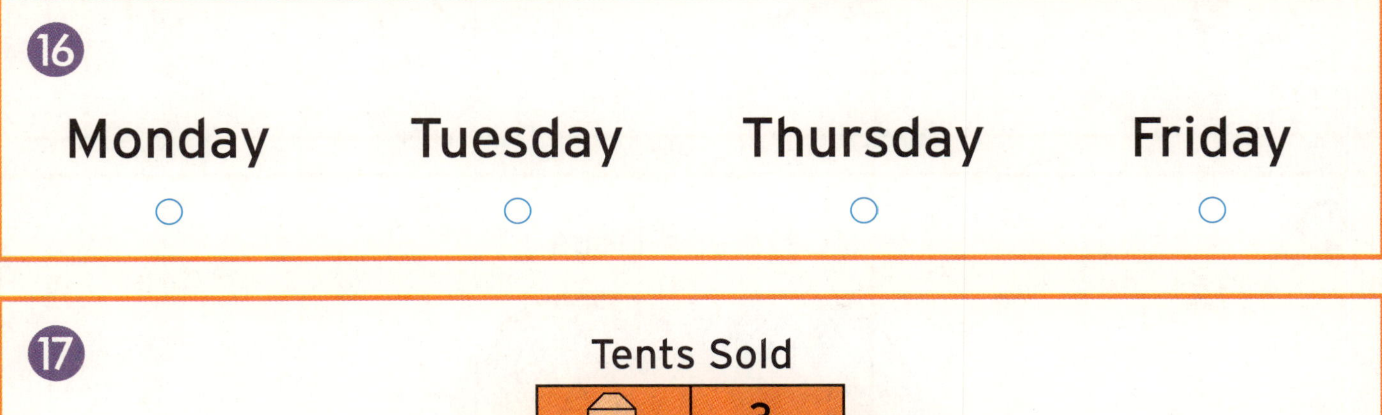

16

Monday ○ Tuesday ○ Thursday ○ Friday ○

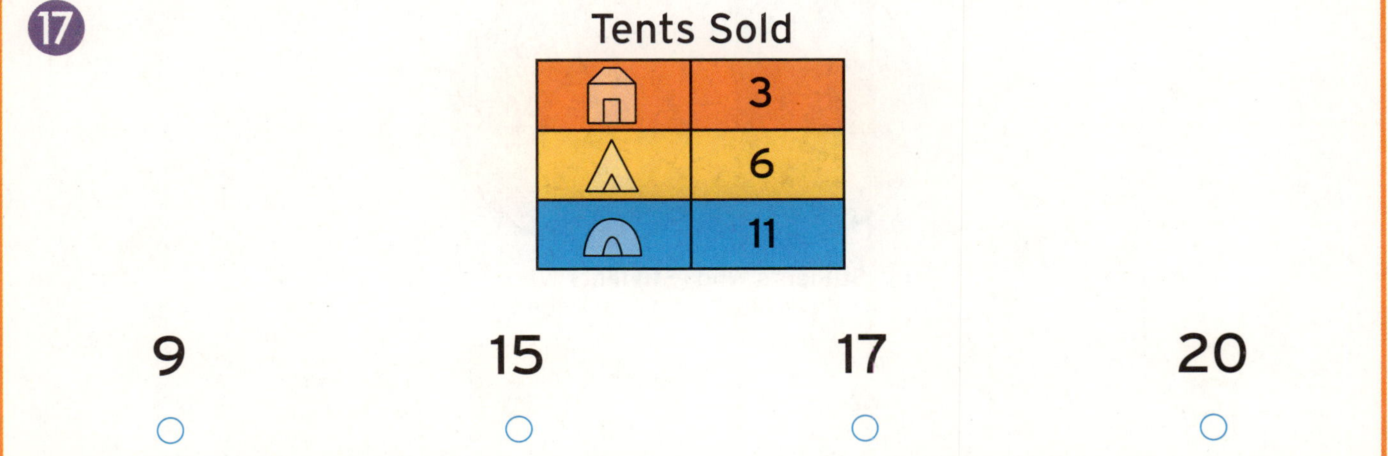

17

Tents Sold

(cabin tent)	3
(pointed tent)	6
(dome tent)	11

9 ○ 15 ○ 17 ○ 20 ○

GO

18
Animals

19
Cats and Dogs
Students Who Have Cats
Students Who Have Dogs
2
4
6
8

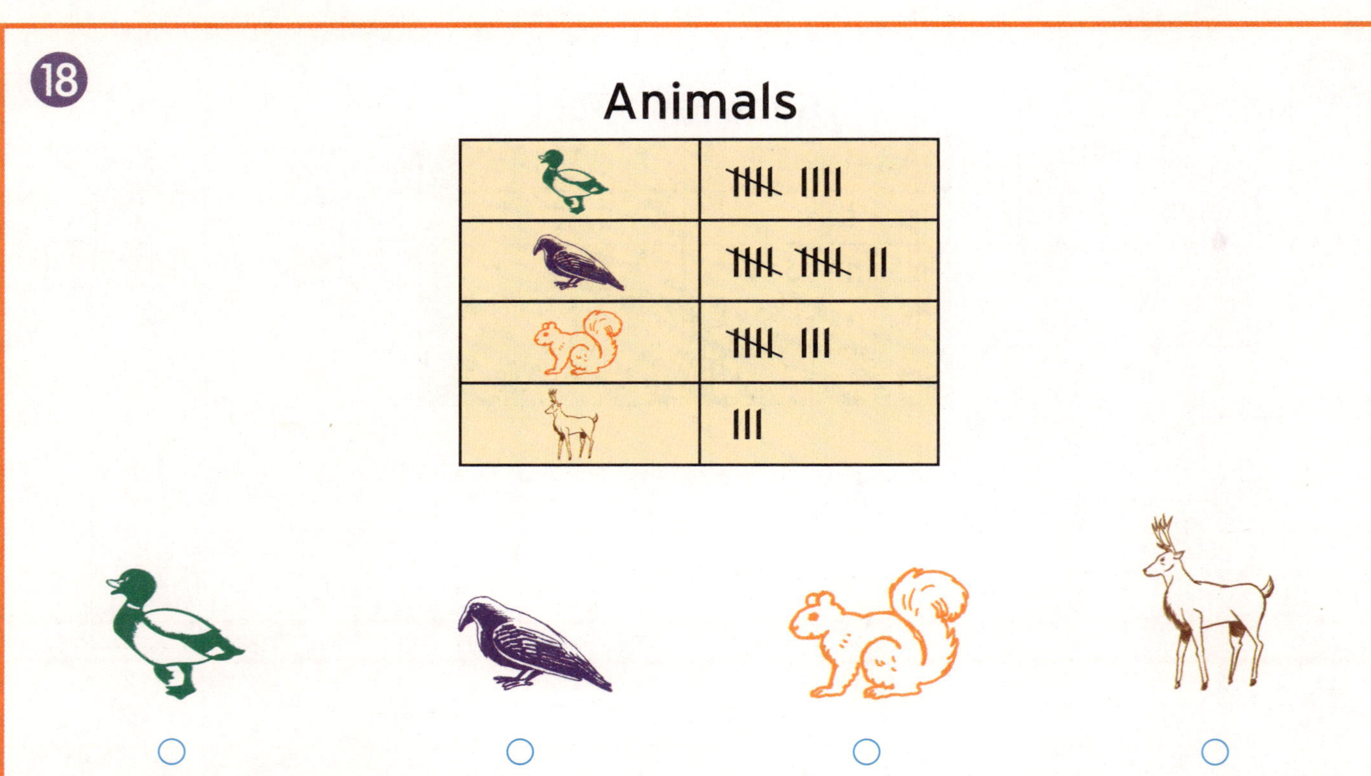

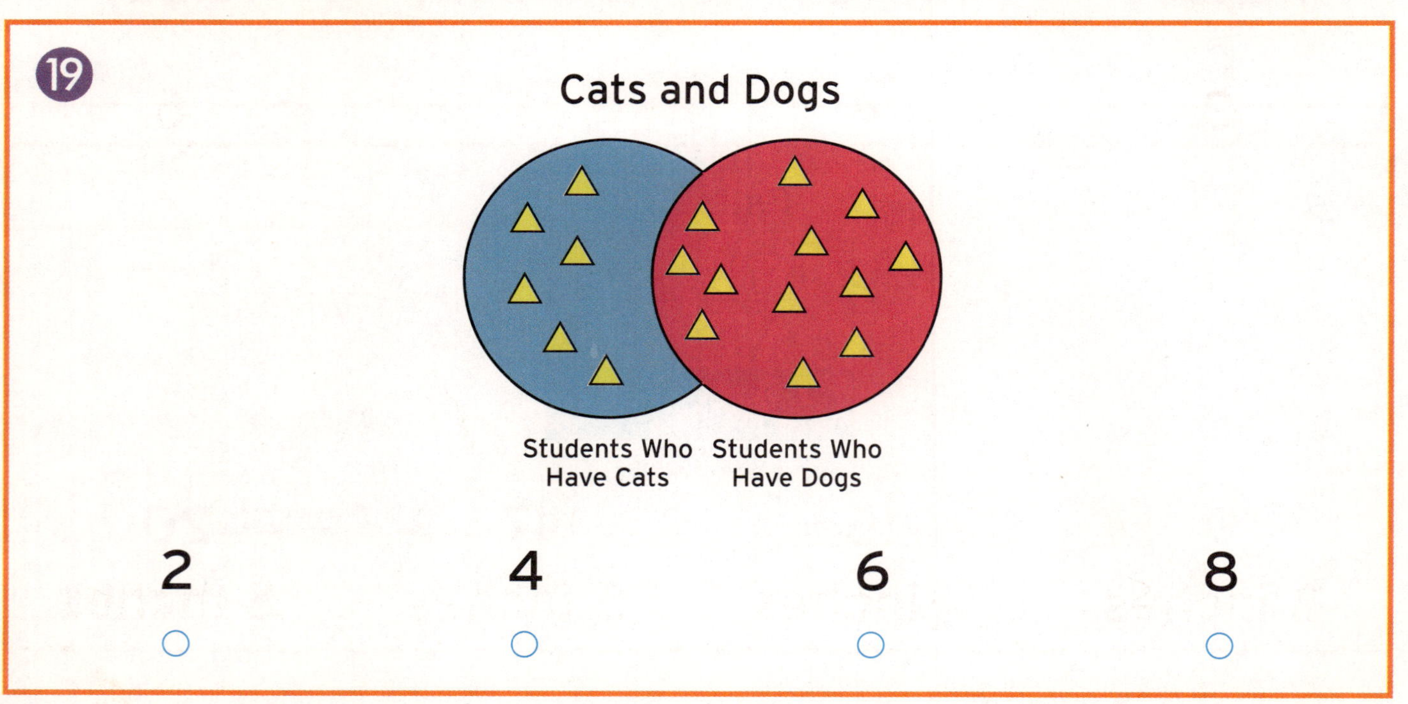

GO

20

○ ○ ○ ○

21

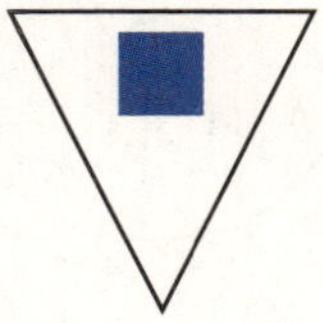

○ ○ ○ ○

22

3 ○ 4 ○ 5 ○ 6 ○

23

3 inches ○ 4 inches ○ 5 inches ○ 6 inches ○

GO

24

pounds ○ gallons ○ cups ○ miles ●

25

○ ○ ○ ●

26

AUGUST

S	M	T	W	T	F	S
				1	2	3
4	5	6	7	8	9	10
11	12	13	14	15	16	17
18	19	20	21	22	23	24
25	26	27	28	29	30	31

August 2 ○ August 7 ○ August 16 ● August 21 ○

STOP

Test Practice

Test 5 **Mathematics Procedures**

SAMPLE A

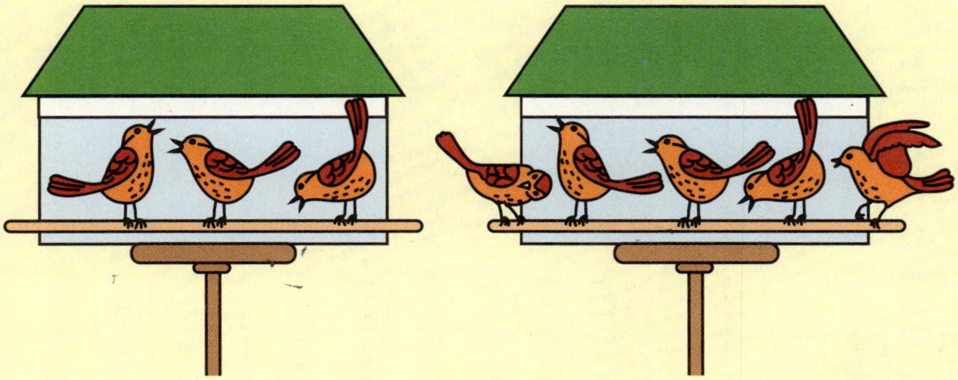

8 ○ 7 ○ 6 ○ NH ○

SAMPLE B

$$9 - 6 = \square$$

2 ○ 4 ○ 15 ○ NH ○

GO

Problem				
1 — 4, 6	8 ○	10 ○	12 ○	NH ○
2 — 11, 5	16 ○	15 ○	14 ○	NH ○
3 — 17, 12	22 ○	27 ○	29 ○	NH ○

GO

4

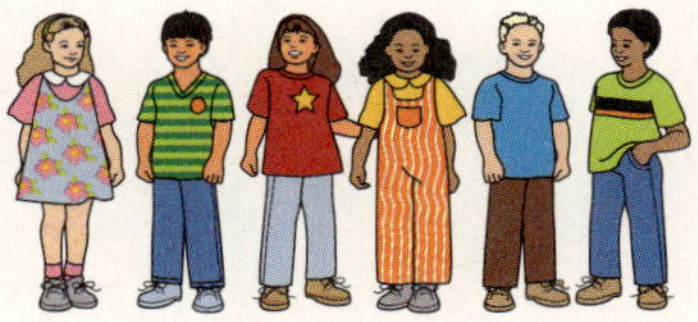

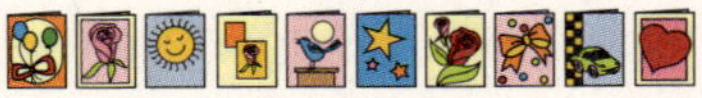

4 ○ | 3 ○ | 2 ○ | NH ○

5

68

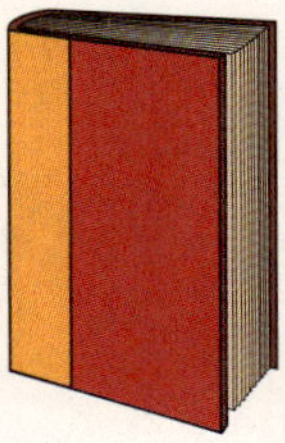

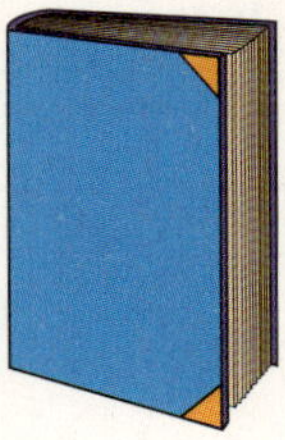

5

73 ○ | 64 ○ | 62 ○ | NH ○

6

45 22

23 ○ | 25 ○ | 27 ○ | NH ○

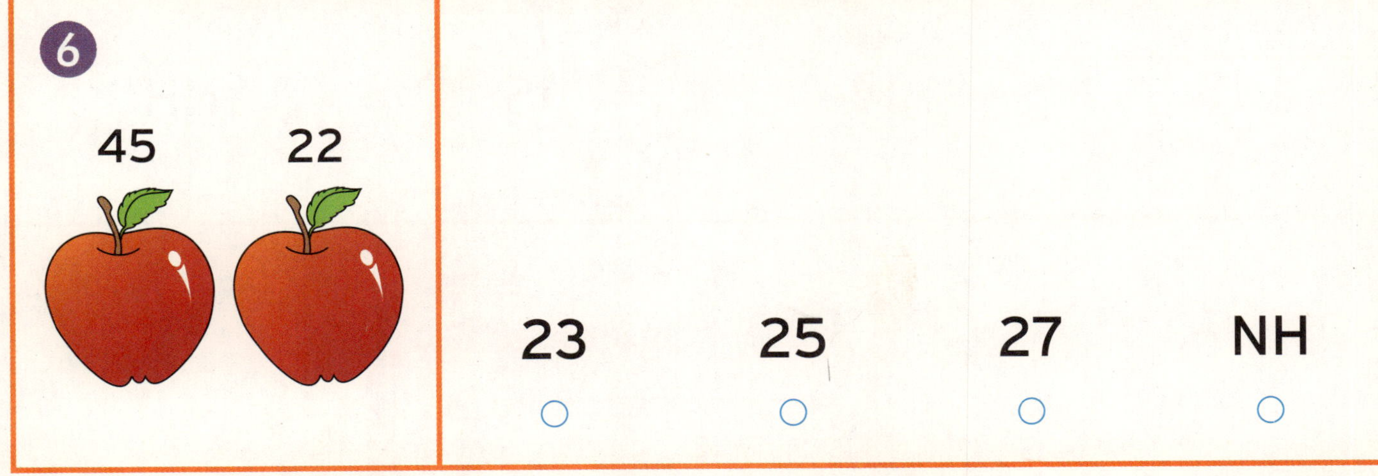

STOP

7

$5 + 8 = \square$

12	13	14	NH
○	○	○	○

8

$4 + 7 = \square$

12	13	14	NH
○	○	○	○

9

$$\begin{array}{r} 6 \\ +\ 8 \\ \hline \end{array}$$

13	14	15	NH
○	○	○	○

GO

10

$$\begin{array}{r} 353 \\ +\ \ 24 \\ \hline \end{array}$$

377 ○ 379 ○ 395 ○ NH ○

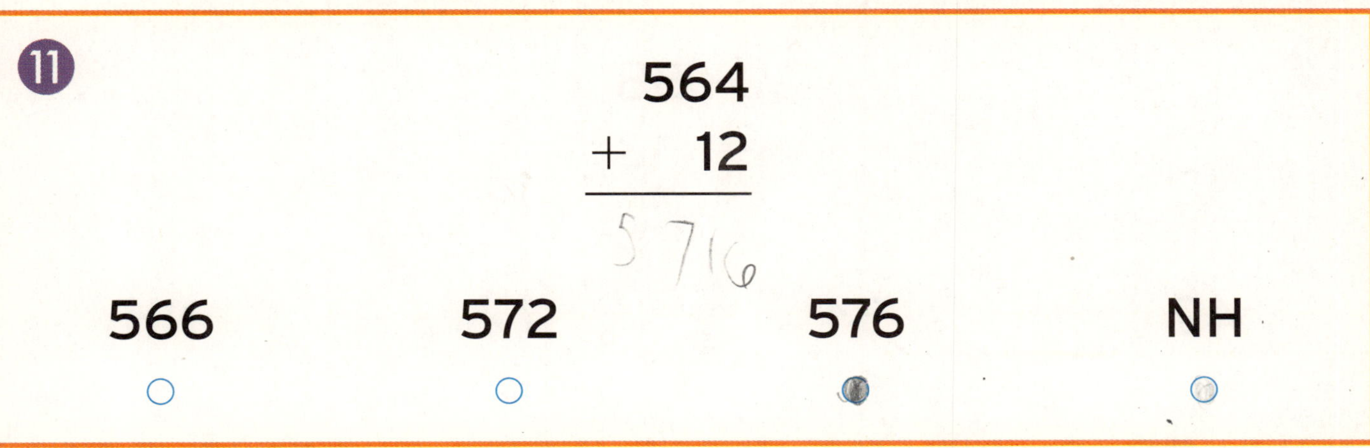

11

$$\begin{array}{r} 564 \\ +\ \ 12 \\ \hline \end{array}$$

566 ○ 572 ○ 576 ○ NH ○

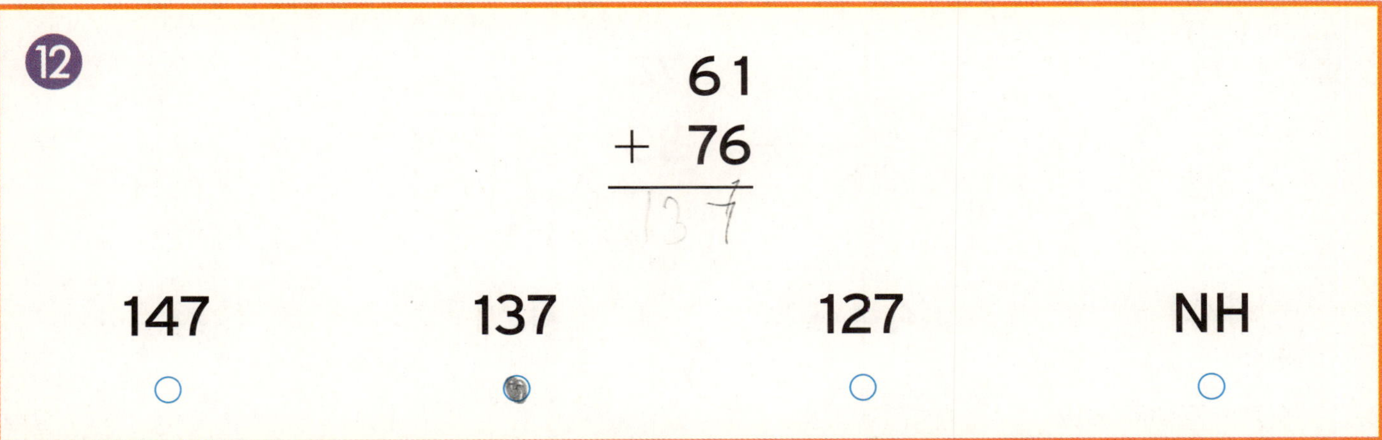

12

$$\begin{array}{r} 61 \\ +\ 76 \\ \hline \end{array}$$

147 ○ 137 ○ 127 ○ NH ○

GO

13

$$\begin{array}{r} 59 \\ -\ 2 \\ \hline \end{array}$$

511

47 ○ 56 ○ 57 ● NH ○

14

$$\begin{array}{r} 58 \\ -\ 13 \\ \hline \end{array}$$

611

42 ○ 54 ○ 72 ○ NH ●

15

$$\begin{array}{r} 474 \\ -\ 33 \\ \hline \end{array}$$

441

441 ● 444 ○ 471 ○ NH ○

STOP 

Unit 9

Test Practice

Test 6 **Spelling**

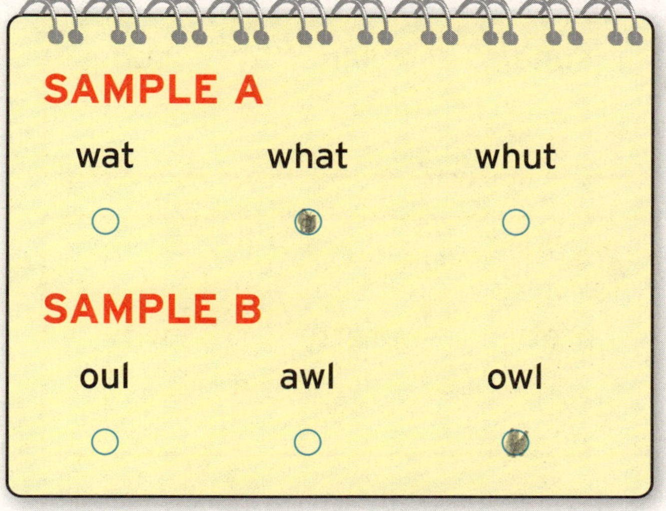

SAMPLE A

wat what whut

SAMPLE B

oul awl owl

1 bizy busy buzy

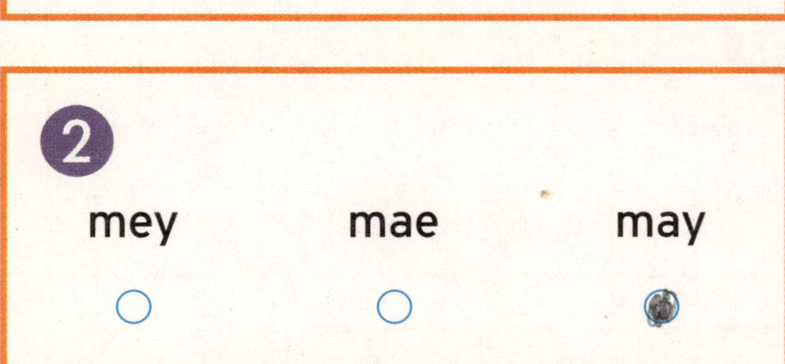

2 mey mae may

3 dayz days deys

4 wone wun one

5 coming comeing comming

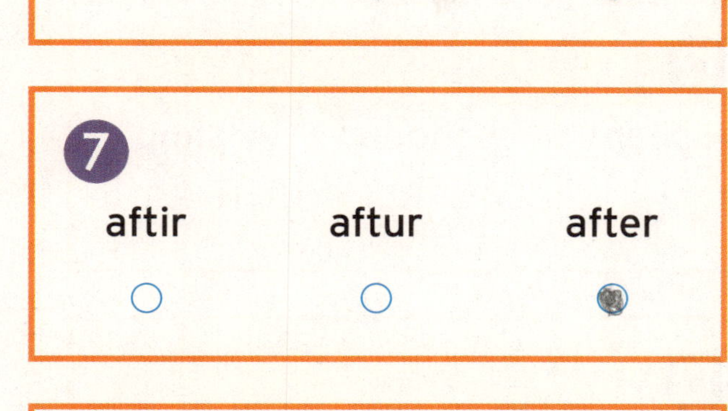

6 parth part pard

7 aftir aftur after

8 fish fich fith

GO

9
hat hut hot
14
sune san sun
10
fut foot fout
15
prety pretty prity
11
push puch pus
16
pin pan pen
12
shap shopp shop
17
aet ayt ate
13
like lick liche
18
pigs pigz piggs

STOP

Test Practice

Test 7 **Language**

SAMPLE A

Do you have a pet.

- ○ Pet!
- ○ pet?
- ○ The way it is

SAMPLE B

My house is very old.

- ○ are
- ○ were
- ○ The way it is

1. We got a new puppy in november.

- ○ november!
- ○ November.
- ○ The way it is

2. Please wash your hands before supper?

- ○ Supper!
- ○ supper.
- ○ The way it is

3. Will the show be over by six o'clock?

- ○ o'clock.
- ○ o'clock!
- ○ The way it is

4. Bill likes eating popcorn as a snack.

- ○ like
- ○ Likes
- ○ The way it is

GO

5 We are having a big party next sunday.

- Sunday.
- sunday!
- The way it is

6 Mara wants to see what it is like in mexico.

- mexico?
- Mexico.
- The way it is

7 The bird sing outside my window every morning.

- sings
- are singing
- The way it is

8 How did you get your new shoes wet!

- Shoes wet.
- shoes wet?
- The way it is

9 "Thanks," said jody after she opened the gift.

- says jody
- said Jody
- The way it is

10 I was born in Kansas City, but then I moved away.

- Kansas city,
- kansas city,
- The way it is

GO

11 Pick a book from the shelf and read it to me.

- ○ me?
- ○ Me!
- ● The way it is

12 You won a prize? That is great news?

- ○ News.
- ● news!
- ○ The way it is

13 He finded an old marble buried in the dirt.

- ● found
- ○ find
- ○ The way it is

14 her cousin goes to dance lessons after school.

- ○ Her cousin go
- ● Her cousin goes
- ○ The way it is

15 Tina looked in the mirror before she left.

- ○ look
- ○ looks
- ● The way it is

16 Evan and Stan sometimes tell each other jokes?

- ○ Jokes!
- ● jokes.
- ○ The way it is

STOP

SAMPLE C

The mouse jumped. Into the hole.

- ○ The mouse jumping into the hole.
- ○ The mouse jumped into the hole.
- ○ The way it is

Erika made a tuna sandwich.

- ○ Erika made. A tuna sandwich.
- ○ Erika making a tuna sandwich.
- ○ The way it is

She was a new player. On the team.

- ○ She was new. Playing on the team.
- ○ She was a new player on the team.
- ○ The way it is

Next week he will plant the corn.

- ○ Next week. He will plant the corn.
- ○ Next week he will plant. The corn.
- ○ The way it is

Elaine carried the old map to school.

- ○ Elaine carrying the old map to school.
- ○ Elaine. She carried the old map to school.
- ○ The way it is

STOP 

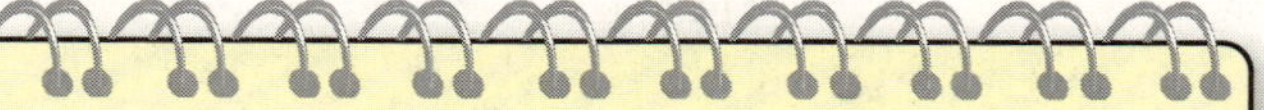

SAMPLE D

Don's grandparents gave him a birthday present.

What should Don write for his grandparents?

- ○ A thank-you letter
- ○ A funny story
- ○ A nice poem

21 Amanda wants to write about her school. She is making a list before she writes her story.

Which of these should be on her list?

- ○ The name of her best friend
- ○ The name of her school
- ○ The name of her street

22 Julia is writing directions about how to bake bread.

Which idea should be first in her directions?

- ○ When to take the bread out of the oven
- ○ How to mix things together
- ○ What things are needed to bake bread

STOP

SAMPLES

Bark is the outside part of most plants and trees. Some trees have thin, smooth bark, while others have thick, rough bark. On your next walk, see how many kinds of bark you can find.

SAMPLE E

Which of these would go best after the last sentence?

- ○ Insects build nests in some trees.
- ○ A park would be a good place to go.
- ○ What plants are in your backyard?

SAMPLE F

Why was this story written?

- ○ To tell where to walk
- ○ To tell what a tree is
- ○ To tell about tree bark

GO

Story 1

Parks are important places in a town or city. They are used in many different ways. Some people go to parks to play or to watch sports. Other people go to parks with their children or to walk their dogs. Some groups hold picnics in parks.

Why was this story written?

- ○ To tell where to have a picnic
- ○ To tell how parks are used
- ○ To tell what sports are played there

Which of these would go best after the last sentence?

- ○ If you built your own park, it would be a special place.
- ○ Do you remember the nicest park you ever visited?
- ○ Parks are playgrounds shared by the people in a city.

GO 

Story 2

Camping trips with my family are special. Two or three times each summer, we drive to the woods. It's an adventure because we stay in a different place every time. One time we camped near a lake. Another time we were close to an old volcano.

Which of these would not go with this story?

- ○ Dad usually picks the spot, but sometimes we help.
- ○ Some people have never been camping before.
- ○ We usually take a truck, a trailer, and a tent.

Which of these would go best after the last sentence?

- ○ The weather is usually good in July and August.
- ○ Mom and Dad camped when they were kids.
- ○ This year we will camp by a place with caves.

STOP

Unit 9

Test Practice

Test 8 **Listening**

SAMPLE A

- ○ lift
- ○ clap
- ○ hold

- ○ hear
- ○ write
- ○ follow

2

- ○ team
- ○ boat
- ○ train

3

- ○ book
- ○ card
- ○ desk

4

- ○ tire
- ○ line
- ○ bend

5

- ○ big
- ○ full
- ○ dark

6

- ○ front
- ○ middle
- ○ side

7

- ○ chair
- ○ bed
- ○ field

GO →

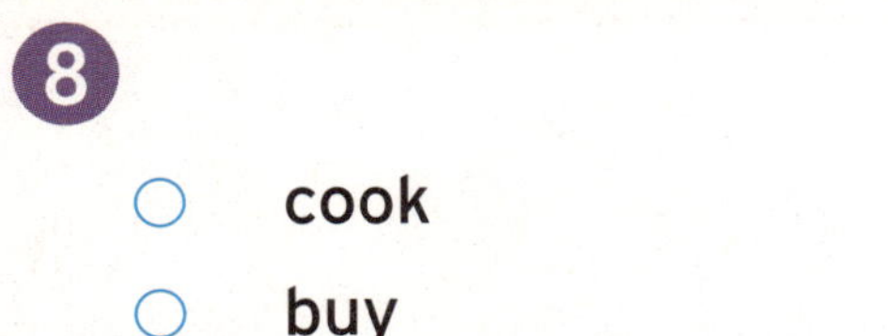

8

- cook
- buy
- cut

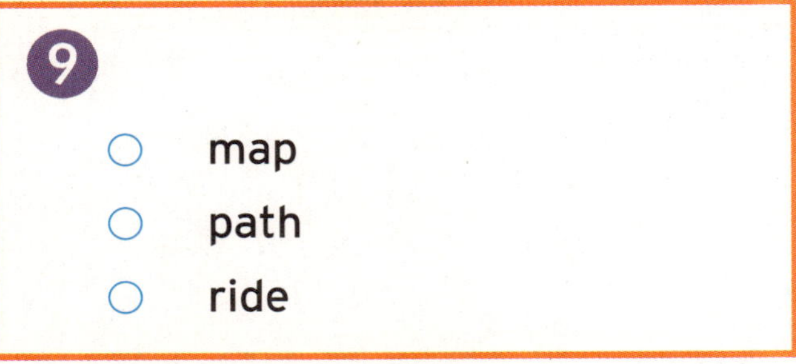

9

- map
- path
- ride

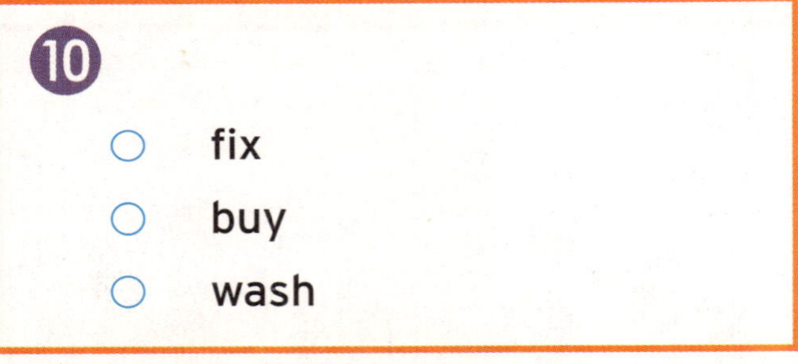

10

- fix
- buy
- wash

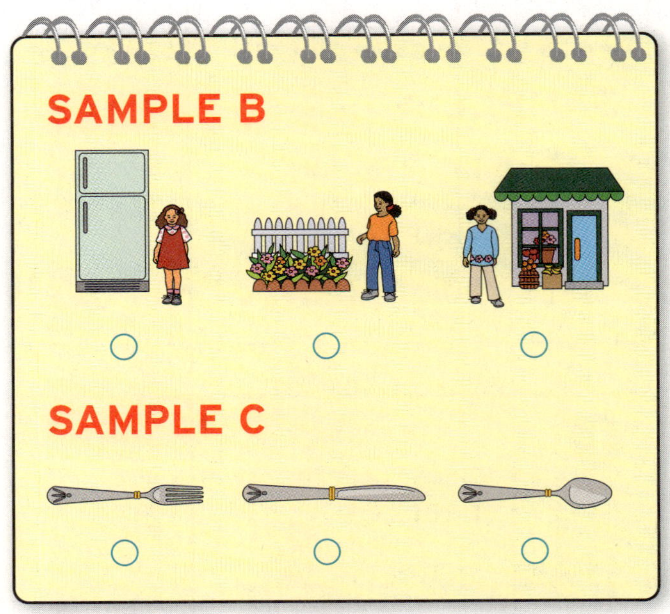

11

12

GO

13

17

14

18

15
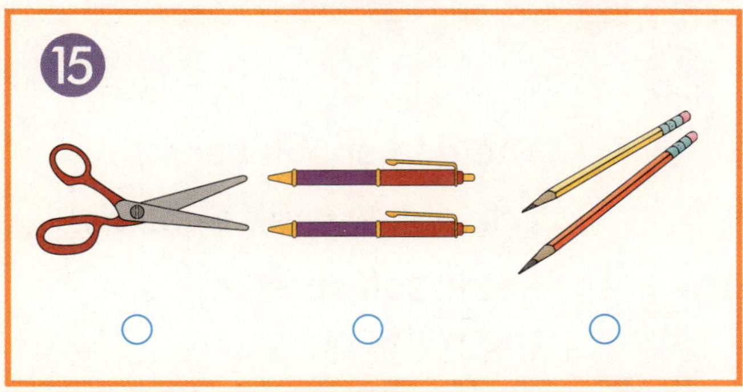

19

16

20

GO

SAMPLE D

- ◯ A tool
- ◯ A rag
- ◯ A drink

SAMPLE E

- ◯ At a table
- ◯ Under a tree
- ◯ In the sun

- ◯ "Where Beetles Live"
- ◯ "All About Beetles"
- ◯ "A Beetle's Body"

- ◯ bugs
- ◯ snails
- ◯ plants

- ◯ It was the family's new dog.
- ◯ The dog was a tiny puppy.
- ◯ The dog was a good swimmer.

- ◯ They wanted to play in the water.
- ◯ They wanted to earn money.
- ◯ Their dad made them.

- ◯ The dog shook herself.
- ◯ Erica blew soap bubbles.
- ◯ Peter splashed in the water.

STOP